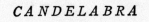

CANDELABRA

CANDELABRA

Selected Essays and Addresses

By

JOHN GALSWORTHY

NEW YORK

CHARLES SCRIBNER'S SONS

1933

AUTHOR'S NOTE

Essays and addresses are supposed to be enlightening; that is why I have called this selection of them "Candelabra." But whether the candles are alight is for the reader rather than myself to judge.

CONTENTS

vii

CONTENTS

*SOME PLATITUDES
CONCERNING DRAMA*

SOME PLATITUDES
CONCERNING DRAMA

A DRAMA must be shaped so as to have a spire of meaning. Every grouping of life and character has its inherent moral; and the business of the dramatist is so to pose the group as to bring that moral poignantly to the light of day. Such is the moral that exhales from plays like *Lear, Hamlet,* and *Macbeth.* But such is not the moral to be found in the great bulk of contemporary Drama. The moral of the average play is now, and probably has always been, the triumph at all costs of a supposed immediate ethical good over a supposed immediate ethical evil.

The vice of drawing these distorted morals has permeated the Drama to its spine; discoloured its art, humanity, and significance; infected its creators, actors, audience, critics; too often turned it from a picture into a caricature. A Drama which lives under the shadow of the distorted moral forgets how to be free, fair, and fine—forgets so completely that it often prides itself on having forgotten.

Now, in writing plays, there are, in this matter of the moral, three courses open to the serious dramatist. The first is: To definitely set before the public that which it wishes to have set before it, the views and codes of life by which the public lives and in which it believes. This way is the most common, successful, and popular. It makes the dramatist's position sure, and not too obviously authoritative.

The second course is: To definitely set before the public those views and codes of life by which the dramatist himself lives, those theories in which he himself believes, the more effectively if they are the opposite of what the public wishes to have placed before it, presenting them so that the audience may swallow them like powder in a spoonful of jam.

There is a third course: To set before the public no cut-and-dried codes, but the phenomena of life and character, selected and combined, *but not distorted,* by the dramatist's outlook, set down without fear, favour, or prejudice, leaving the public to draw such poor moral as nature may afford. This third method requires a certain detachment; it requires a sympathy with, a love of, and a curiosity as to, things for their own sake; it requires a far view, together with patient industry, for no immediately practical result.

It was once said of Shakespeare that he had never done any good to any one, and never would. This, unfortunately, could not, in the sense in which the word "good" was then meant, be said of most modern dramatists. In truth, the good that Shakespeare did to humanity was of a remote, and, shall we say, eternal nature; something of the good that men get from having the sky and the sea to look at. And this partly because he was, in his greater plays at all events, free from the habit of drawing a distorted moral. Now, the playwright who supplies to the public the facts of life distorted by the moral which it expects, does so

4

that he may do the public what he considers an immediate good, by fortifying its prejudices; and the dramatist who supplies to the public facts distorted by his own advanced morality, does so because he considers that he will at once benefit the public by substituting for its worn-out ethics, his own. In both cases the advantage the dramatist hopes to confer on the public is immediate and practical.

But matters change, and morals change; men remain—and to set men, and the facts about them, down faithfully so that they draw for us the moral of their natural actions, may also possibly be of benefit to the community. It is, at all events, harder than to set men and facts down, as they ought, or ought not to be. This, however, is not to say that a dramatist should or indeed can, keep himself and his temperamental philosophy out of his work. As a man lives and thinks, so will he write. But it is certain, that to the making of good drama, as to the practice of every other art, there must be brought an almost passionate love of discipline, a white-heat of self-respect, a desire to make the truest, fairest, best thing in one's power; and that to these must be added an eye that does not flinch. Such qualities alone will bring to a drama the selfless character which soaks it with inevitability.

The word "pessimist" is frequently applied to the few dramatists who have been content to work in this way. It has been applied, among others, to Euripides, to Shakespeare, to Ibsen; it will be applied to many in the future. Nothing, however, is more dubious than

5

the way in which these two words "pessimist" and "optimist" are used; for the optimist appears to be he who cannot bear the world as it is, and is forced by his nature to picture it as it ought to be, and the pessimist one who cannot only bear the world as it is, but loves it well enough to draw it faithfully. The true lover of the human race is surely he who can put up with it in all its forms, in vice as well as in virtue, in defeat no less than in victory; the true seer he who sees not only joy but sorrow, the true painter of human life one who blinks at nothing. It may be that he is also, incidentally, its true benefactor.

In the whole range of the social fabric there are only two impartial persons, the scientist and the artist, and under the latter heading such dramatists as desire to write not only for to-day, but for to-morrow, must strive to come.

But dramatists being as they are made—past remedy—it is perhaps more profitable to examine the various points at which their qualities and defects are shown.

The plot! A good plot is that sure edifice which slowly rises out of the interplay of circumstance on temperament, and temperament on circumstance, within the enclosing atmosphere of an idea. A human being is the best plot there is; it may be impossible to see why he is a good plot, because the idea within which he was brought forth cannot be fully grasped; but it is plain that *he is a good plot*. He is organic. And so it must be with a good play. Reason alone produces no good plots; they come by original sin, sure conception, and instinctive after-power of selecting what benefits the germ. A bad plot, on the other hand, is simply a row of stakes, with a character impaled on each—characters who would have liked to live, but came to untimely grief; who started bravely, but fell on these stakes, placed beforehand in a row, and were transfixed one by one, while their ghosts stride on, squeaking and gibbering, through the play. Whether these stakes are made of facts or of ideas, according to the nature of the dramatist who planted them, their effect on the unfortunate characters is the same; the creatures were begotten to be staked, and staked they are! The demand for a good plot, not unfrequently heard, commonly signifies: "Tickle my sensations by stuffing the play with arbitrary adventures, so that I need not be troubled to take the characters seriously. Set the persons of the play to action, regardless of time, sequence, atmosphere, and probability!"

Now, true dramatic action is what characters do, at once contrary, as it were, to expectation, and yet because they have already done other things. No dramatist should let his audience know what is coming; but neither should he suffer his characters to act without making his audience feel that those actions are in harmony with temperament, and arise from previous known actions, together with the temperaments and previous known actions of the other characters in the play. The dramatist who hangs his characters to his plot, instead of hanging his plot to his characters, is guilty of cardinal sin.

7

The dialogue! Good dialogue again is character, marshalled so as continually to stimulate interest or excitement. The reason good dialogue is seldom found in plays is merely that it is hard to write, for it requires not only a knowledge of what interests or excites, but such a feeling for character as brings misery to the dramatist's heart when his creations speak as they should not speak—ashes to his mouth when they say things for the sake of saying them— disgust when they are "smart."

The art of writing true dramatic dialogue is an austere art, denying itself all license, grudging every sentence devoted to the mere machinery of the play, suppressing all jokes and epigrams severed from character, relying for fun and pathos on the fun and tears of life. From start to finish good dialogue is hand-made, like good lace; clear, of fine texture, furthering with each thread the harmony and strength of a design to which all must be subordinated.

But good dialogue is also spiritual action. In so far as the dramatist divorces his dialogue from spiritual action—that is to say, from progress of events, or toward events which are significant of character—he is stultifying τὸ δρᾶμα the thing done; he may make pleasing disquisitions, he is not making drama. And in so far as he twists character to suit his moral or his plot, he is neglecting a first principle, that truth to nature which alone invests art with hand-made quality.

The dramatist's license, in fact, ends with his design. In conception alone he is free. He may take

8

what character or group of characters he chooses, see
them with what eyes, knit them with what idea, within
the limits of his temperament; but once taken, seen,
and knitted, he is bound to treat them like a gentleman, with the tenderest consideration of their mainsprings. Take care of character; action and dialogue
will take care of themselves! The true dramatist gives
full rein to his temperament in the scope and nature
of his subject; having once selected subject and characters, he is just, gentle, restrained, neither gratify-
ing his lust for praise at the expense of his offspring,
nor using them as puppets to flout his audience. Being
himself the nature that brought them forth, he guides
them in the course predestined at their conception. So
only have they a chance of defying Time, which is
always lying in wait to destroy the false, topical, or
fashionable, all—in a word—that is not based on the
permanent elements of human nature. The perfect
dramatist rounds up his characters and facts within
the ring-fence of a dominant idea which fulfils the
craving of his spirit; having got them there, he suffers them to live their own lives.

Plot, action, character, dialogue! But there is yet
another subject for a platitude. Flavour! An impalpa-
ble quality, less easily captured than the scent of a
flower, the peculiar and most essential attribute of
any work of art! It is the thin, poignant spirit which
hovers up out of a play, and is as much its differen-
tiating essence as is caffeine of coffee. Flavour, in
fine, is the spirit of the dramatist projected into his
work in a state of volatility, so that no one can ex-

9

actly lay hands on it, here, there, or anywhere. This distinctive essence of a play, marking its brand, is the one thing at which the dramatist cannot work, for it is outside his consciousness. A man may have many moods, he has but one spirit; and this spirit he communicates in some subtle, unconscious way to all his work. It waxes and wanes with the currents of his vitality, but no more alters than a chestnut changes into an oak.

For, in truth, dramas are very like unto trees, springing from seedlings, shaping themselves inevitably in accordance with the laws fast hidden within themselves, drinking sustenance from the earth and air, and in conflict with the natural forces round them. So they slowly come to full growth, until warped, stunted, or risen to fair and gracious height, they stand open to all the winds. And the trees that spring from each dramatist are of different race; he is the spirit of his own sacred grove, into which no stray tree can by any chance enter.

One more platitude. It is not unfashionable to pit one form of drama against another—holding up the naturalistic to the disadvantage of the epic; the epic to the belittlement of the fantastic; the fantastic to the detriment of the naturalistic. Little purpose is thus served. The essential meaning, truth, beauty, and irony of things may be revealed under all these forms. Vision over life and human nature can be as keen and just, the revelation as true, inspiring, delight-giving, and thought-provoking, whatever fashion be employed—it is simply a question of doing it well enough to uncover the kernel of the nut. Whether the violet come from Russia, from Parma, or from England, matters little. Close by the Greek temples at Paestum there are violets that seem redder, and sweeter, than any ever seen—as though they have sprung up out of the footprints of some old pagan goddess; but under the April sun, in a Devonshire lane, the little blue scentless violets capture every bit as much of the spring. And so it is with drama—no matter what its form—it need only be the "real thing," need only have caught some of the precious fluids, revelation, or delight, and imprisoned them within a chalice to which we may put our lips and continually drink.

And yet, starting from this last platitude, one may perhaps be suffered to speculate as to the particular forms that our renascent drama is likely to assume. For our drama is renascent, and nothing will stop its growth. It is not renascent because this or that man is writing, but because of a new spirit. A spirit that is no doubt in part the gradual outcome of the impact on our home-grown art, of Russian, French, and Scandinavian influences, but which in the main rises from an awakened humanity in the conscience of our time.

What, then, are to be the main channels down which the renascent English drama will float in the coming years? It is more than possible that these main channels will come to be two in number and situate far apart.

The one will be the broad and clear-cut channel of

naturalism, down which will course a drama poignantly shaped, and inspired with high intention, but faithful to the seething and multiple life around us, drama such as some are inclined to term photographic, deceived by a seeming simplicity into forgetfulness of the old proverb, "Ars est celare artem," and oblivious of the fact, that, to be vital, to grip, such drama is in every respect as dependent on imagination, construction, selection, and elimination—the main laws of artistry—as ever was the romantic or rhapsodic play. The question of naturalistic technique will bear, indeed, much more study than has yet been given to it. The aim of the dramatist employing it is obviously to create such an illusion of actual life passing on the stage as to compel the spectator to pass through an experience of his own, to think, and talk, and move with the people he sees thinking, talking, and moving in front of him. A false phrase, a single word out of tune or time, will destroy that illusion and spoil the surface as surely as a stone heaved into a still pool shatters the image seen there. But this is only the beginning of the reason why the naturalistic is the most exacting and difficult of all techniques. It is easy enough to *reproduce* the exact conversation and movements of persons in a room; it is desperately hard to *produce* the perfectly natural conversation and movements of those persons, when each natural phrase spoken and each natural movement made has not only to contribute toward the growth and perfection of a drama's soul, but also to be a revelation, phrase by phrase, movement by movement, of essential traits of character. To put it another way, naturalistic art, when alive, indeed to be alive at all, is simply the art of manipulating a procession of most delicate symbols. Its service is the swaying and focusing of men's feelings and thoughts in the various departments of human life. It will be like a steady lamp, held up from time to time, in whose light things will be seen for a space clearly and in due proportion, freed from the mists of prejudice and partisanship.

And the other of these two main channels will, I think, be a twisting and delicious stream, which will bear on its breast new barques of poetry, shaped, it may be, like prose, but a prose incarnating through its fantasy and symbolism all the deeper aspirations yearning, doubts, and mysterious stirrings of the human spirit; a poetic prose-drama, emotionalising us by its diversity and purity of form and invention, and whose province will be to disclose the elemental soul of man and the forces of Nature, not perhaps as the old tragedies disclosed them, not necessarily in the epic mood, but always with beauty and in the spirit of discovery.

Such will, I think, be the two vital forms of our drama in the coming generation. And between these two forms there must be no crude unions; they are too far apart, the cross is too violent. For, where there is a seeming blend of lyricism and naturalism, it will on examination be found, I think, to exist only in plays whose subjects or settings—as in Synge's "Playboy of the Western World," or in Mr. Masefield's "Nan"—are so removed from our ken that we cannot really tell, and therefore do not care, whether an absolute illusion is maintained. The poetry which may and should exist in naturalistic drama, can only be that of perfect rightness of proportion, rhythm, shape—the poetry, in fact, that lies in all vital things. It is the ill-mating of forms that has killed a thousand plays. We want no more bastard drama; no more attempts to dress out the simple dignity of every-day life in the peacock's feathers of false lyricism; no more straw-stuffed heroes or heroines; no more rabbits and goldfish from the conjurer's pockets, nor any limelight. Let us have starlight, moonlight, sunlight, and the light of our own self-respects.

1909.

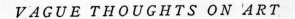

VAGUE THOUGHTS ON ART

I T was on a day of rare beauty that I went out into the fields to try and gather these few thoughts. So golden and sweetly hot it was, that they came lazily, and with a flight no more coherent or responsible than the swoop of the very swallows; and, as in a play or poem, the result is conditioned by the conceiving mood, so I knew would be the nature of my diving, dipping, pale-throated, fork-tailed words. But, after all—I thought, sitting there—I need not take my critical pronouncements seriously. I have not the firm soul of the critic. It is not my profession to know things for certain, and to make others feel that certainty. On the contrary, I am often wrong—a luxury no critic can afford. And so, invading as I was the realm of others, I advanced with a light pen, feeling that none, and least of all myself, need expect me to be right.

What then—I thought—is Art? For I perceived that to think about it I must first define it; and I almost stopped thinking at all before the fearsome nature of that task. Then slowly in my mind gathered this group of words:

Art is that imaginative expression of human energy, which, through technical concretion of feeling and perception, tends to reconcile the individual with the universal, by exciting in him impersonal emotion. And the greatest Art is that which excites the greatest impersonal emotion in an hypothetical perfect human being.

Impersonal emotion! And what—I thought—do I mean by that? Surely I mean: That is *not* Art, which, while I am contemplating it, inspires me with any active or directive impulse; that *is* Art, when, for however brief a moment, it replaces within me interest in myself by interest in itself. For, let me suppose myself in the presence of a carved marble bath. If my thoughts be: "What could I buy that for?" Impulse of acquisition; or: "From what quarry did it come?" Impulse of inquiry; or: "Which would be the right end for my head?" Mixed impulse of inquiry and acquisition—I am at that moment insensible to it as a work of Art. But, if I stand before it vibrating at sight of its colour and forms, if ever so little and for ever so short a time, unhaunted by any definite practical thought or impulse—to that extent and for that moment it has stolen me away out of myself and put itself there instead; has linked me to the universal by making me forget the individual in me. And for that moment, and only while that moment lasts, it is to me a work of Art. The word "impersonal," then, is but used in this my definition to signify momentary forgetfulness of one's own personality and its active wants.

So Art—I thought—is that which, heard, read, or looked on, while producing no directive impulse, warms one with unconscious vibration. Nor can I imagine any means of defining what is the greatest Art, without hypotheticating a perfect human being. But since we shall never see, or know if we do see, that desirable creature—dogmatism is banished, "Academy" is dead to the discussion, deader than ever Tolstoi left it after his famous treatise "What is Art?" for, having destroyed all the old Judges and Academies, Tolstoi, by saying that the greatest Art was that which appealed to the greatest number of living human beings, raised up the masses of mankind to be a definite new Judge or Academy, as tyrannical and narrow as ever were those whom he had destroyed.

This, at all events—I thought—is as far as I dare go in defining what Art is. But let me try to make plain to myself what is the essential quality that gives to Art the power of exciting this unconscious vibration, this impersonal emotion. It has been called Beauty! An awkward word—a perpetual begging of the question; too current in use, too ambiguous altogether; now too narrow, now too wide—a word, in fact, too glib to know at all what it means. And how dangerous a word—often misleading us into slabbing with extraneous floridities what would otherwise, on its own plane, be Art! To be decorative where decoration is not suitable, to be lyrical where lyricism is out of place, is assuredly to spoil Art, not to achieve it. But this essential quality of Art has also, and more happily, been called Rhythm. And, what is Rhythm if not that mysterious harmony between part and part, and part and whole, which gives what is called life; that exact proportion, the mystery of which is best grasped in observing how life abandons an animate creature when the essential relation of part to whole has been sufficiently disturbed. And I agree that this rhythmic relation of part to part, and part to whole—in short, vitality—is the one quality inseparable from a work of Art. For nothing which does not seem to a man possessed of this rhythmic vitality, can ever steal him out of himself.

And having got thus far in my thoughts, I paused, watching the swallows; for they seemed to me the symbol, in their swift, sure curvetting, all daring and balance and surprise, of the delicate poise and motion of Art, that visits no two men alike, in a world where no two things of all the things there be, are quite the same.

Yes—I thought—and this Art is the one form of human energy in the whole world, which really works for union, and destroys the barriers between man and man. It is the continual, unconscious replacement, however fleeting, of one self by another self; the real cement of human life; the everlasting refreshment and renewal. For, what is grievous, dompting, grim, about our lives is that we are shut up within ourselves, with an itch to get outside ourselves. And to be stolen away from ourselves by Art is a momentary relaxation from that itching, a minute's profound, and as it were secret, enfranchisement. The active amusements and relaxations of life can only rest certain of our faculties, by indulging others; the whole self is never rested save in that unconsciousness of self, which comes through rapt contemplation of Nature or of Art.

And suddenly I remembered that some believe that Art does not produce unconsciousness of self, but rather very vivid self-realisation.

Yes, but—I thought—that is not the first and instant effect of Art; the new impetus is the after effect of that momentary replacement of oneself by the self of the work before us; it is surely *the result* of that brief span of enlargement, enfranchisement, and rest.

So, Art is the great and universal refreshment. For Art is never dogmatic; holds no brief for itself—you may take it or you may leave it. It does not force itself rudely where it is not wanted. It is reverent to all tempers, to all points of view. But it is wilful—the very wind in the comings and goings of its influence, an uncapturable fugitive, visiting our hearts at vagrant, sweet moments; since we often stand even before the greatest works of Art without being able quite to lose ourselves! That restful oblivion comes, we never quite know when—and it is gone! But when it comes, it is a spirit hovering with cool wings, blessing us from least to greatest, according to our powers; a spirit deathless and varied as human life itself.

And in what sort of age—I thought—are artists living now? Are conditions favourable? Life is very multiple; full of "movements," "facts," and "news"; with the limelight terribly turned on—and all this is adverse to the artist. Yet, leisure is abundant; the facilities for study great; Liberty is respected—more or less. But, there is one great reason why, in this age of ours, Art, it seems, must flourish. For, just as cross-breeding in Nature—if it be not too violent—

often gives an extra vitality to the offspring, so does cross-breeding of philosophies make for vitality in Art. I cannot help thinking that historians, looking back from the far future, will record this age as the Third Renaissance. We who are lost in it, working or looking on, can neither tell what we are doing, nor where standing; but we cannot help observing, that, just as in the Greek Renaissance, worn-out Pagan orthodoxy was penetrated by new philosophy; just as in the Italian Renaissance, Pagan philosophy, reasserting itself, fertilized again an already too inbred Christian creed; so now Orthodoxy fertilized by Science is producing a fresh and fuller conception of life—a love of Perfection, not for hope of reward, not for fear of punishment, but for Perfection's sake. Slowly, under our feet, beneath our consciousness, is forming that new philosophy, and it is in times of new philosophies that Art, itself in essence always a discovery, must flourish. Those whose sacred suns and moons are ever in the past, tell us that our Art is going to the dogs; and it is, indeed, true that we are in confusion! The waters are broken, and every nerve and sinew of the artist is strained to discover his own safety. It is an age of stir and change, a season of new wine and old bottles. Yet, assuredly, in spite of breakages and waste, a wine worth the drinking is all the time being made.

I ceased again to think, for the sun had dipped low, and the midges were biting me; and the sounds of evening had begun, those innumerable far-travelling sounds of man and bird and beast—so clear and inti-

mate—of remote countryside at sunset. And for long
I listened, too vague to move my pen.

New philosophy—a vigorous Art! Are there not
all the signs of it? In music, sculpture, painting; in
fiction—and drama; in dancing; in criticism itself,
if criticism be an Art. Yes, we are reaching out to
a new faith not yet crystallized, to a new Art not yet
perfected; the forms still to find—the flowers still to
fashion!

And how has it come, this slowly growing faith in
Perfection for Perfection's sake? Surely like this:
The Western world awoke one day to find that it no
longer believed corporately and for certain in future
life for the individual consciousness. It began to feel:
I cannot say more than that there may be such. Death
may be the end of man, or Death may be nothing. And
it began to ask itself in this uncertainty: Do I then
desire to go on living? Now, since it found that it
desired to go on living at least as earnestly as ever
it did before, it began to inquire why. And slowly it
perceived that there was, inborn within it, a passionate instinct of which it had hardly till then been conscious—a sacred instinct to perfect itself, now, as well
as in a possible hereafter; to perfect itself because
Perfection was desirable, a vision to be adored, and
striven for; a dream motive fastened within the
Universe; the very essential Cause of everything.
And it began to see that this Perfection, cosmically,
was nothing but perfect Equanimity and Harmony;
and in human relations, nothing but perfect Love and
Justice. And Perfection began to glow before the

23

eyes of the Western world like a new star, whose light touched with glamour all things as they came forth from Mystery, till to Mystery they were ready to return.

This—I thought—is surely what the Western world has dimly been rediscovering. There has crept into our minds once more the feeling that the Universe is all of a piece, Equipoise supreme; and all things equally wonderful, and mysterious, and valuable. We have begun, in fact, to have a glimmering of the artist's creed, that nothing may we despise or neglect—that everything is worth the doing well, the making fair—that our God, Perfection, is implicit everywhere, and the revelation of Him the business of our Art.

And as I jotted down these words I noticed that some real stars had crept up into the sky, so gradually darkening above the pollard lime-trees; cuckoos, who had been calling on the thorn-trees all the afternoon, were silent; the swallows no longer flirted past, but a bat was already in career over the holly hedge; and round me the buttercups were closing. The whole form and feeling of the world had changed, so that I seemed to have before me a new picture hanging.

Art—I thought—must indeed be priest of this new faith in Perfection, whose motto is: "Harmony, Proportion, Balance." For by Art alone can true harmony in human affairs be fostered, true Proportion revealed, and true Equipoise preserved. Is not the training of an artist a training in the due relation of one thing to another, and in the faculty of expressing that relation clearly; and, even more, a training in the faculty of disengaging from self the very essence of self—and passing that essence into other selves by so delicate means that none shall see how it is done, yet be insensibly unified? Is not the artist, of all men, foe and nullifier of partisanship and parochialism, of distortions and extravagance, the discoverer of that jack-o'-lantern—Truth; for, if Truth be not Spiritual Proportion I know not what it is. Truth—it seems to me—is no absolute thing, but always relative, the essential symmetry in the varying relationships of life; and the most perfect truth is but the concrete expression of the most penetrating vision. Life seen throughout as a countless show of the finest works of Art; Life shaped, and purged of the irrelevant, the gross, and the extravagant; Life, as it were, spiritually selected—that is Truth; a thing as multiple and changing, as subtle, and strange, as Life itself, and as little to be bound by dogma. Truth admits but the one rule : No deficiency, and no excess ! Disobedient to that rule—nothing attains full vitality. And secretly fettered by that rule is Art, whose business is the creation of vital things.

That æsthete, to be sure, was right, when he said: "It is style that makes one believe in a thing; nothing but Style." For, what is Style in its true and broadest sense save fidelity to idea and mood, and perfect balance in the clothing of them? And I thought: Can one believe in the decadence of Art in an age which, however unconsciously as yet, is beginning to worship that which Art worships—Perfection—Style?

25

The faults of our Arts to-day are the faults of zeal and of adventure, the faults and crudities of pioneers, the errors and mishaps of the explorer. They must pass through many fevers, and many times lose their way; but at all events they shall not go dying in their beds, and be buried at Kensal Green. And, here and there, amid the disasters and wreckage of their voyages of discovery, they will find something new, some fresh way of embellishing life, or of revealing the heart of things. That characteristic of to-day's Art—the striving of each branch of Art to burst its own boundaries—which to many spells destruction, is surely of happy omen. The novel straining to become the play, the play the novel, both trying to paint; music striving to become story; poetry gasping to be music; painting panting to be philosophy; forms, canons, rules, all melting in the pot; stagnation broken up! In all this havoc there is much to shock and jar even the most eager and adventurous. We cannot stand these new-fangled fellows! They have no form! They rush in where angels fear to tread. They have lost all the good of the old, and given us nothing in its place! And yet—only out of stir and change is born new salvation. To deny that is to deny belief in man, to turn our backs on courage! It is well, indeed, that some should live in closed studies with the paintings and the books of yesterday—such devoted students serve Art in their own way. But the fresh-air world will ever want new forms. We shall not get them without faith enough to risk the old! The good will live, the bad will die; and to-morrow only can tell us which is which!

Yes—I thought—we naturally take a too impatient view of the Art of our own time, since we can neither see the ends toward which it is almost blindly groping, nor the few perfected creations that will be left standing amidst the rubble of abortive effort. An age must always decry itself and extol its forbears. The unwritten history of every Art will show us that. Consider the novel—that most recent form of Art! Did not the age which followed Fielding lament the treachery of authors to the Picaresque tradition, complaining that they were not as Fielding and Smollett were? Be sure they did. Very slowly and in spite of opposition did the novel attain in this country the fullness of that biographical form achieved under Thackeray. Very slowly, and in face of condemnation, it has been losing that form in favour of a greater vividness which places before the reader's brain, not historical statements, as it were, of motives and of facts, but word-paintings of things and persons, so chosen and arranged that the reader may see, as if at first hand, the spirit of Life at work before him. The new novel has as many bemoaners as the old novel had when it was new. It is no question of better or worse, but of *differing* forms—of change dictated by gradual suitability to the changing conditions of our social life, and to the ever fresh discoveries of craftsmen, in the intoxication of which, old and equally worthy craftsmanship is—by the way —too often for the moment mislaid. The vested in-

27

terests of life favour the line of least resistance—
disliking and revolting against disturbance; but one
must always remember that a spurious glamour is
inclined to gather around what is new. And, because
of these two deflecting factors, those who break
through old forms must well expect to be dead before the new forms they have unconsciously created
have found their true level, high, or low, in the world
of Art. When a thing is new—how shall it be judged?
In the fluster of meeting novelty, we have even seen
coherence attempting to bind together two personalities so fundamentally opposed as those of Ibsen and
Bernard Shaw—dramatists with hardly a quality in
common; no identity of tradition, or belief; not the
faintest resemblance in methods of construction or
technique. Yet contemporary estimate talks of them
often in the same breath. They are new! It is enough.
And others, as utterly unlike them both. They too are
new. They have as yet no label of their own—then
put on some one else's!

And so—I thought—it must always be; for Time
is essential to the proper placing and estimate of all
Art. And is it not this feeling, that contemporary
judgments are apt to turn out a little ludicrous, which
has converted much criticism of late from judgment
pronounced into impression recorded—recreative
statement—a kind, in fact, of expression of the critic's self, elicited through contemplation of a book, a
play, a symphony, a picture? For this kind of criticism
there has even recently been claimed an actual identity
with creation. Æsthetic judgment and creative power

identical! That is a hard saying. For, however sympathetic one may feel toward this new criticism, however one may recognize that the recording of impression has a wider, more elastic, and more lasting value than the delivery of arbitrary judgment based on rigid laws of taste; however one may admit that it approaches the creative gift in so far as it demands the qualities of receptivity and reproduction—is there not still lacking to this "new" critic something of that thirsting spirit of discovery, which precedes the creation—hitherto so-called—of anything? Criticism, taste, æsthetic judgment, by the very nature of their task, wait till life has been focussed by the artists before they attempt to reproduce the image which that imprisoned fragment of life makes on the mirror of their minds. But a thing created springs from a germ unconsciously implanted by the direct impact of unfettered life on the whole range of the creator's temperament; and round the germ thus engendered, the creative artist—ever penetrating, discovering, selecting—goes on building cell on cell, gathered from a million little fresh impacts and visions. And to say that this is also exactly what the recreative critic does, is to say that the interpretative musician is creator in the same sense as is the composer of the music that he interprets. If, indeed, these processes be the same in kind, they are in degree so far apart that one would think the word creative unfortunately used of both.

But this speculation—I thought—is going beyond the bounds of vagueness. Let there be some thread of coherence in your thoughts, as there is in the progress of this evening, fast fading into night. Return to the consideration of the nature and purposes of Art! And recognize that much of what you have thought will seem on the face of it heresy to the school whose doctrine was incarnated by Oscar Wilde in that admirable apotheosis of half-truth: "The Decay of the Art of Lying." For therein he said: "No great artist ever sees things as they really are." Yet, that half-truth might also be put thus: The seeing of things as they really are—the seeing of a proportion veiled from other eyes (together with the power of expression), is what makes a man an artist. What makes him a great artist is a high fervour of spirit, which produces a superlative, instead of a comparative, clarity of vision.

Close to my house there is a group of pines with gnarled red limbs flanked by beech-trees. And there is often a very deep blue sky behind. Generally, that is all I see. But, once in a way, in those trees against that sky I seem to see all the passionate life and glow that Titian painted into his pagan pictures. I have a vision of mysterious meaning, of a mysterious relation between that sky and those trees with their gnarled red limbs and Life as I know it. And when I have had that vision I always feel, this is reality, and all those other times, when I have no such vision, simple unreality. If I were a painter, it is for such fervent vision I should wait, before moving brush. This, so intimate, inner vision of reality, indeed, seems in duller moments well nigh grotesque; and hence that other glib half-truth: "Art is greater than

Life itself." Art *is,* indeed, greater than Life in the
sense that the power of Art is the disengagement
from Life of its real spirit and significance. But in
any other sense, to say that Art is greater than Life
from which it emerges, and into which it must re-
merge, can but suspend the artist over Life, with his
feet in the air and his head in the clouds—Prig mas-
querading as Demi-god. "Nature is no great Mother
who has borne us. She is our creation. It is in our
brain that she quickens to life." Such is the highest
hyperbole of the æsthetic creed. But what is creative
instinct, if not an incessant living sympathy with
Nature, a constant craving like that of Nature's own,
to fashion something new out of all that comes within
the grasp of those faculties with which Nature has
endowed us? The qualities of vision, of fancy, and
of imaginative power, are no more divorced from
Nature, than are the qualities of common-sense and
courage. They are rarer, that is all. But in truth, no
one holds such views. Not even those who utter them.
They are the rhetoric, the over-statement of half-
truths, by such as wish to condemn what they call
"Realism," without being temperamentally capable
of understanding what "Realism" really is.

And what—I thought—is Realism? What is the
meaning of that word so wildly used? Is it descriptive
of technique, or descriptive of the spirit of the artist;
or both, or neither? Was Turgenev a realist? No
greater poet ever wrote in prose, nor any one who
more closely brought the actual shapes of men and
things before us. No more fervent idealists than

31

Ibsen and Tolstoi ever lived; and none more careful
to make their people real. Were they realists? No
more deeply fantastic writer can I conceive than
Dostoievsky, nor any who has described actual situa-
tions more vividly. Was he a realist? The late Stephen
Crane was called a realist. Than whom no more impressionistic writer ever painted with words. What
then is the heart of this term still often used as an
expression almost of abuse? To me, at all events—I
thought—the words realism, realistic, have no longer
reference to technique, for which the words naturalism, naturalistic, serve far better. Nor have they to
do with the question of imaginative power—as much
demanded by realism as by romanticism. For me, a
realist is by no means tied to naturalistic technique
—he may be poetic, idealistic, fantastic, impressionistic, anything but—romantic; that, in so far as he is
a realist, he cannot be. The word, in fact, character-
izes that artist whose temperamental preoccupation
is with revelation of the actual interrelating spirit of
life, character, and thought, with a view to *enlighten*
himself and others; as distinguished from that artist
—whom I call romantic—whose temperamental purpose is invention of tale or design with a view to
delight himself and others. It is a question of temperamental antecedent motive in the artist, and nothing more.

Realist—Romanticist! Enlightenment—Delight!
That is the true apposition. To make a revelation—
to tell a fairy-tale! And either of these artists may
use what form he likes—naturalistic, fantastic, po-

etic, impressionistic. For it is not by the form, but by the purpose and mood of his art that he shall be known, as one or as the other. Realists indeed—including the half of Shakespeare that was realist— not being primarily concerned to amuse their audience, are still comparatively unpopular in a world made up for the greater part of men of action, who instinctively reject all art that does not distract them without causing them to think. For thought makes demands on an energy already in full use; thought causes introspection; and introspection causes discomfort, and disturbs the grooves of action. To say that the object of the realist is to enlighten rather than to delight, is not to say that in his art the realist is not amusing himself as much as ever is the teller of a fairy-tale, though he does not deliberately start out to do so; he is amusing, too, a large part of mankind. For, admitted that the object, and the test of Art, is always the awakening of vibration, of impersonal emotion, it is still usually forgotten that men fall, roughly speaking, into two flocks: Those whose intelligence is uninquiring in the face of Art, and does not demand to be appeased before their emotions can be stirred; and those who, having a speculative bent of mind, must first be satisfied by an enlightening quality in a work of Art, before that work of Art can awaken in them feeling. The audience of the realist is drawn from this latter type of man; the much larger audience of the romantic artist from the former; together with, in both cases, those fastidious few for whom all Art is style and only style, and who welcome either kind, so long as it is good enough.

To me, then—I thought—this division into Realism and Romance, so understood, is the main cleavage in all the Arts; but it is hard to find pure examples of either kind. For even the most determined realist has more than a streak in him of the romanticist, and the most resolute romanticist finds it impossible at times to be quite unreal. Guido Reni, Watteau, Leighton—were they not perhaps somewhat pure romanticists; Rembrandt, Hogarth, Manet—mainly realists; Botticelli, Titian, Raphael, a blend? Dumas père, and Scott, surely romantic; Flaubert and Tolstoi as surely realists; Dickens and Cervantes, blended. Keats and Swinburne—romantic; Browning and Whitman—realistic; Shakespeare and Goethe, both. The Greek dramatists—realists. The Arabian Nights and Malory—romantic. The Iliad, the Odyssey, and the Old Testament, both realism and romance. And if in the vagueness of my thoughts I were to seek for illustration less general and vague to show the essence of this temperamental cleavage in all Art, I would take the two novelists Turgenev and Stevenson. For Turgenev expressed himself in stories that must be called romances, and Stevenson employed almost always a naturalistic technique. Yet no one would ever call Turgenev a romanticist, or Stevenson a realist. The spirit of the first brooded over life, found in it a perpetual voyage of spiritual adventure, was set on discovering and making clear to himself and all, the varying traits and emotions of human character—the varying moods of Nature; and though he couched all this discovery in caskets of engaging story, it was always clear as day what mood it was that drove him to dip pen in ink. The spirit of the second, I think, almost dreaded to discover; he felt life, I believe, too keenly to want to probe into it; he spun his gossamer to lure himself and all away from life. That was his driving mood; but the craftsman in him, longing to be clear and poignant, made him more natural, more actual than most realists.

So, how thin often is the hedge! And how poor a business the partisan abuse of either kind of art in a world where each sort of mind has full right to its own due expression, and grumbling lawful only when due expression is not attained! One may not care for a Rembrandt portrait of a plain old woman; a graceful Watteau decoration may leave another cold—but foolish will he be who denies that both are faithful to their conceiving moods, and so proportioned part to part, and part to whole, as to have, each in its own way, that inherent rhythm or vitality which is the hall-mark of Art. He is but a poor philosopher who holds a view so narrow as to exclude forms not to his personal taste. No realist can love romantic Art so much as he loves his own, but when that Art fulfils the laws of its peculiar being, if he would be no blind partisan, he must admit it. The romanticist will never be amused by realism, but let him not for that reason be so parochial as to think that realism, when it achieves vitality, is not Art. For what is Art but the perfected expression of self in contact with the world; and whether that

self be of enlightening, or of fairy-telling temperament, is of no moment whatsoever. The tossing of
abuse from realist to romanticist and back is but the
sword-play of two one-eyed men with their blind
side turned toward each other. Shall not each attempt be judged on its own merits? If found not
shoddy, faked, or forced, but true to itself, true to
its conceiving mood, and fair-proportioned part to
whole, so that it *lives*—then, realistic or romantic,
in the name of Fairness let it pass! Of all kinds of
human energy, Art is surely the most free, the least
parochial; and demands of us an essential tolerance
of all its forms. Shall we waste breath and ink in
condemnation of artists, because their temperaments
are not our own?

But the shapes and colours of the day were now
all blurred; every tree and stone entangled in the
dusk. How different the world seemed from that in
which I had first sat down, with the swallows flirt-
ing past. And my mood was different; for each of
those worlds had brought to my heart its proper
feeling—painted on my eyes the just picture. And
Night, that was coming, would bring me yet another
mood that would frame itself with consciousness at
its own fair moment, and hang before me. A quiet
owl stole by in the field below, and vanished into
the heart of a tree. And suddenly above the moor-
line I saw the large moon rising. Cinnamon-coloured,
it made all things swim, made me uncertain of my
thoughts, vague with mazy feeling. Shapes seemed
but drifts of moon-dust, and true reality nothing

save a sort of still listening to the wind. And for long I sat, just watching the moon creep up, and hearing the thin, dry rustle of the leaves along the holly hedge. And there came to me this thought: What is this Universe—that never had beginning and will never have an end—but a myriad striving to perfect pictures never the same, so blending and fading one into another, that all form one great perfected picture? And what are we—ripples on the tides of a birthless, deathless, equipoised Creative Purpose—but little works of Art?

Trying to record that thought, I noticed that my notebook was damp with dew. The cattle were lying down. It was too dark to see.

1911.

MEDITATION ON FINALITY

MEDITATION ON FINALITY

In the Grand Canyon of Arizona, that most exhilarating of all natural phenomena, Nature has for once so focussed her effects, that the result is a framed and final work of Art. For there, between two high lines of plateau, level as the sea, are sunk the wrought thrones of the innumerable gods, couchant, and for ever revering, in their million moods of light and colour, the Master Mystery.

Having seen this culmination, I realize why many people either recoil before it, and take the first train home, or speak of it as a "remarkable formation." For, though mankind at large craves finality, it does not crave the sort that bends the knee to Mystery. In Nature, in Religion, in Art, in Life, the common cry is: "Tell me precisely where I am, what doing, and where going! Let me be free of this fearful untidiness of not knowing all about it!" The favoured religions are always those whose message is most finite. The fashionable professions—those that end us in assured positions. The most popular works of fiction, such as leave nothing to our imagination. And to this craving after prose, who would not be lenient, if he has at all known life, with its usual predominance of our lower and less courageous selves, our constant hankering after the cosy closed door and line of least resistance? We are continually begging to be allowed to know for certain; though, if our prayer were granted, and Mystery no longer hovered, made blue the hills, and turned day into night, we should, as surely, wail at once to be delivered of that ghastliness of knowing things for certain!

Now, in Art, I would never quarrel with a certain living writer who demands of it the kind of finality implied in what he calls a "moral discovery" —using, no doubt, the words in their widest sense. I would maintain, however, that such finality is not confined to positively discovering the true conclusion of premises laid down; but that it may also distil gradually, negatively from the whole work, in a moral discovery, as it were, of Author. In other words, that permeation by an essential point of view, by emanation of author, may so unify and vitalize a work, as to give it all the finality that need be required of Art. For the finality that is requisite to Art, be it positive or negative, is not the finality of dogma, nor the finality of fact, it is ever the finality of feeling—of a spiritual light, subtly gleaned by the spectator out of that queer luminous haze which one man's nature must ever be to others. And herein, incidentally, it is that Art acquires also that quality of mystery, more needful to it even than finality, for the mystery that wraps a work of Art is the mystery of its maker, and the mystery of its maker is the difference between that maker's soul and every other soul.

But let me take an illustration of what I mean by these two kinds of finality that Art may have, and show that in essence they are but two halves of the same thing. The term "a work of Art" will not be denied, I think, to that early novel of M. Anatole France, "Le Lys Rouge." Now, that novel has *positive* finality, since the spiritual conclusion from its premises strikes one as true. But neither will the term "a work of Art" be denied to the same writer's four "Bergeret" volumes, whose *negative* finality consists only in the temperamental atmosphere wherein they are soaked. Now, if the theme of "Le Lys Rouge" had been treated by Tolstoi, Meredith, or Turgenev, we should have had spiritual conclusions from the same factual premises so different from M. France's as prunes from prisms, and yet, being the work of equally great artists, they would, doubtless, have struck us as equally true. Is not, then, the positive finality of "Le Lys Rouge," though expressed in terms of a different craftsmanship, the same, in essence, as the negative finality of the "Bergeret" volumes? Are not both, in fact, merely flower of author true to himself? So long as the scent, colour, form of that flower is strong and fine enough to affect the senses of our spirit, then all the rest, surely, is academic—I would say, immaterial.

But here, in regard to Art, is where mankind at large comes on the field. " 'Flower of author,' " it says, " 'Senses of the spirit!' Phew! Give me some-

43

thing I can understand! Let me know where I am getting to!" In a word, it wants a finality different from that which Art can give. It will ask the artist, with irritation, what his solution, or his lesson, or his meaning, really is, having omitted to notice that the poor creature has been giving all the meaning that he can, in every sentence. It will demand to know why it was not told definitely what became of Charles or Mary in whom it had grown so interested; and will be almost frightened to learn that the artist knows no more than itself. And if by any chance it be required to dip its mind into a philosophy that does not promise it a defined position both in this world and the next, it will assuredly recoil, and with a certain contempt say: "No, sir! This means nothing to me; and if it means anything to you—which I very much doubt—I am sorry for you!"

It must have facts, and again facts, not only in the present and the past, but in the future. And it demands facts of that, which alone cannot glibly give it facts. It goes on asking facts of Art, or, rather, such facts as Art cannot give—for, after all, even "flower of author" is fact in a sort of way.

Consider, for instance, Synge's masterpiece, "The Playboy of the Western World!" There is flower of author! What is it for mankind at large? An attack on the Irish character! A pretty piece of writing! An amusing farce! Enigmatic cynicism leading nowhere! A puzzling fellow wrote it! Mankind at large has little patience with puzzling fellows.

Few, in fact, want flower of author. Moreover, it

is a quality that may well be looked for where it does
not exist. To say that the finality which Art requires
is merely an enwrapping mood, or flower of author,
is not by any means to say that any robust fellow,
slamming his notions down in ink, can give us these.
Indeed, no! So long as we see the author's proper
person in his work, we do not see the flower of him.
Let him retreat himself, if he pretend to be an artist.
There is no less of subtle skill, no less impersonality,
in the "Bergeret" volumes than in "Le Lys Rouge."
No less labour and mental torturing went to their
making, page by page, in order that they might exhale their perfume of mysterious finality, their withdrawn but implicit judgment. Flower of author is
not quite so common as the buttercup, the Califor-
nian poppy, or the gay Texan galliardia, and for
that very reason the finality it gives off will never
be robust enough for a mankind at large that would
have things cut and dried, and labelled in thick letters. For, consider—to take one phase alone of this
demand for factual finality—how continual and in-
sistent is the cry for characters that can be worshipped; how intense and persistent the desire to be
told that Charles was a real hero; and how bitter the
regret that Mary was no better than she should be!
Mankind at large wants heroes that are heroes, and
heroines that are heroines—and nothing so inappro-
priate to them as unhappy endings.

Travelling away, I remember, from that Grand
Canyon of Arizona were a young man and a young
woman, evidently in love. He was sitting very close

to her, and reading aloud for her pleasure, from a paper-covered novel, heroically oblivious of us all:

" 'Sir Robert,' she murmured, lifting her beauteous eyes, 'I may not tempt you, for you are too dear to me!' Sir Robert held her lovely face between his two strong hands. 'Farewell!' he said, and went out into the night. But something told them both that, when he had fulfilled his duty, Sir Robert would return. . . ." He had not returned before we reached the Junction, but there was finality about that baronet, and we well knew that he ultimately would. And, long after the sound of that young man's faithful reading had died out of our ears, we meditated on Sir Robert, and compared him with the famous characters of fiction, slowly perceiving that they were none of them so final in their heroism as he. No, none of them reached that apex. For Hamlet was a most unfinished fellow, and Lear extremely violent; Pickwick addicted to punch, and Sam Weller to fibbing; Bazarov actually a Nihilist, and Irina—! Levin and Anna, Pierre and Natasha, all of them stormy and unsatisfactory at times. "Un Cœur Simple" nothing but a servant, and an old maid at that; "Saint Julien l'Hospitalier" a sheer fanatic. Colonel Newcome too irritable and too simple altogether. Don Quixote certified insane. Hilda Wangel, Nora, Hedda—Sir Robert would never even have spoken to such baggages! Monsieur Bergeret—an amiable weak thing! D'Artagnan—a true swashbuckler! Tom Jones, Faust, Don Juan—we might not even think of them. And those poor

46

Greeks: Prometheus—shocking rebel. Œdipus—for a long time banished by the Censor. Phædra and Elektra, not even so virtuous as Mary, who failed of being what she should be! And coming to more familiar persons—Joseph and Moses, David and Elijah, all of them lacked his finality of true hero-ism—none could quite pass muster beside Sir Rob-ert. . . . Long we meditated, and, reflecting that an author must ever be superior to the creatures of his brain, were refreshed to think that there were so many living authors capable of giving birth to Sir Robert; for indeed, Sir Robert and finality like his —no doubtful heroes, no flower of author, and no mystery—is what mankind at large has always want-ed from Letters, and will always want.

As truly as that oil and water do not mix, there are two kinds of men. The main cleavage in the whole tale of life is this subtle, all-pervading divi-sion of mankind into the man of facts and the man of feeling. And not by what they are or do can they be told one from the other, but just by their atti-tude toward finality. Fortunately most of us are nei-ther quite the one nor quite the other. But between the pure-blooded of each kind there is real antipathy, far deeper than the antipathies of race, politics, or religion—an antipathy that not circumstance, love, goodwill, or necessity will ever quite get rid of. Sooner shall the panther agree with the bull than that other one with the man of facts. There is no bridging the gorge that divides these worlds.

Nor is it so easy to tell, of each, to which world

he belongs, as it was to place the lady, who held out her finger over that gorge called Grand Canyon, and said:

"It doesn't look thirteen miles; but they measured it just there! Excuse my pointing!"

1912.

DIAGNOSIS OF THE ENGLISHMAN

DIAGNOSIS OF THE
ENGLISHMAN

FIRST let it be said that there is no more unconsciously deceptive person on the face of the globe. The Englishman does not know himself; outside England he is but guessed at.

Racially the Englishman is so complex and so old a blend that no one can say what he is. In character he is just as complex. Physically, there are two main types; one inclining to length of limb, narrowness of face and head (you will see nowhere such long and narrow heads as in our islands), and bony jaws; the other approximating more to the ordinary "John Bull." The first type is gaining on the second. There is little or no difference in the main character behind.

In attempting to understand the real nature of the Englishman, certain salient facts must be borne in mind.

THE SEA.—To be surrounded generation after generation by the sea has developed in him a suppressed idealism, a peculiar impermeability, a turn for adventure, a faculty for wandering, and for being sufficient unto himself in far and awkward surroundings.

THE CLIMATE.—Whoso weathers for centuries a climate that, though healthy and never extreme, is, perhaps, the least reliable and one of the wettest in the world, must needs grow in himself a counter-

51

balance of dry philosophy, a defiant humour, an enforced medium temperature of soul. The Englishman is no more given to extremes than is his climate; against its damp and perpetual changes he has become coated with a sort of bluntness.

THE POLITICAL AGE OF HIS COUNTRY.—This is by far the oldest settled Western Power, politically speaking. For eight hundred and fifty years England has known no serious military disturbance from without; for nearly two hundred she has known no serious political turmoil within. This is partly the outcome of her isolation, partly the happy accident of her political constitution, partly the result of the Englishman's habit of looking before he leaps, which comes, no doubt, from the climate and the mixture of his blood. This political stability has been a tremendous factor in the formation of English character, has given the Englishman of all ranks a certain deep slow sense of form and order, an engrained culture, if one may pirate the word—that makes no show, being in the bones of the man, as it were.

THE GREAT PREPONDERANCE FOR SEVERAL GENERATIONS OF TOWN OVER COUNTRY LIFE.—Taken in conjunction with centuries of political stability, this is the main cause of a growing inarticulate humaneness, of which—speaking generally—the Englishman appears to be rather ashamed.

THE PUBLIC SCHOOLS.—This potent element in the formation of the modern Englishman, not only in the upper but in all classes, is something that one rather despairs of making understood—in countries which have no similar institution. But! Imagine one hundred thousand youths of the wealthiest, healthiest, and most influential classes, passed, during each generation, at the most impressionable age, into a sort of ethical mould, emerging therefrom stamped to the core with the impress of an uniform morality, uniform manners, uniform way of looking at life; remembering always that these youths fill seven-eights of the important positions in the professional administration of their country and the conduct of its commercial enterprise; remembering too, that, through perpetual contact with every other class, their standard of morality and way of looking at life filter down into the very toes of the land. This great character-forming machine is remarkable for an un-self-consciousness which gives it enormous strength and elasticity. Not inspired by the State, it inspires the State. The characteristics of the philosophy it enjoins are mainly negative, and, for that, the stronger. "Never show your feelings—to do so is not manly, and bores your fellows. Don't cry out when you're hurt, making yourself a nuisance to other people. Tell no tales about your companions and no lies about yourself. Avoid all 'swank,' 'side,' 'swagger,' braggadocio of speech or manner, on pain of being laughed at." (This maxim is carried to such a pitch that the Englishman, except in his Press, habitually understates everything.)

"Think little of money, and speak less of it. Play games hard, and keep the rules of them, even when your blood is hot and you are tempted to disregard them. In three words: PLAY THE GAME"—a little phrase which may be taken as the characteristic understatement of the modern Englishman's creed of honour, in all classes. This potent, unconscious machine has great defects. It tends to the formation of "caste"; it is a poor teacher of sheer learning; and æsthetically, with its universal suppression of all interesting and queer individual traits of personality —it is almost horrid. Yet it imparts a remarkable incorruptibility to English life; it conserves vitality, by suppressing all extremes; and it implants everywhere a kind of unassuming stoicism and respect for the rules of the great game—Life. Through its unconscious example, and through its cult of games, it has vastly influenced even the classes not directly under its control.

Three more main facts must be borne in mind:——

ESSENTIAL DEMOCRACY OF GOVERNMENT.

FREEDOM OF SPEECH AND THE PRESS.

ABSENCE HITHERTO OF COMPULSORY MILITARY
    SERVICE.

These, the outcome of the quiet and stable home life of an island people, have done more than anything to make the Englishman a deceptive personality to the outside eye. He has for centuries been licensed to grumble. There is no such confirmed grumbler— until he really has something to grumble at; and then, no one perhaps who grumbles less. There is no such confirmed carper at the condition of his country, yet no one really so profoundly convinced that it is the best in the world. A stranger might well think from his utterances that he was spoiled by the freedom of his life, unprepared to sacrifice anything for a land in such a condition. Threaten that country, and with it his liberty, and you will find that his grumbles have meant less than nothing. You will find, too, that behind the apparent slackness of every arrangement and every individual are powers of adaptability to facts, elasticity, practical genius, a spirit of competition amounting almost to disease, and a determination, that are staggering. Before the Great War began, it was the fashion among a number of English to lament the decadence of the race. Those very grumblers became foremost in praising the spirit shown in every part of their country. Their lamentations, which plentifully deceived the outside ear, were just English grumbles; for if, in truth, England had been decadent, there could have been no universal display for them to have praised. All this democratic grumbling, and habit of "going as you please," serve a deep purpose. Autocracy, Censorship, Compulsion, destroy humour in a nation's blood and elasticity in its fibre; they cut at the very mainsprings of national vitality. Only if reasonably free from control can a man really arrive at what is or is not national necessity, and truly identify himself with a national ideal by simple conviction from within.

Two words of caution to strangers trying to form an estimate of the Englishman: He must not be judged from his Press, which, manned (with certain exceptions) by those who are not typically English, is much too-highly-coloured to illustrate the true English spirit; nor can he be judged from his literature.

The Englishman is essentially inexpressive, unexpressed. Further, he must not be judged by the evidence of his wealth. England may be the richest country in the world per head of population, but not five per cent of that population have any wealth to speak of, certainly not enough to have affected their hardihood; and, with inconsiderable exceptions, those who have enough are brought up to worship hardihood.

From these main premises, then, we come to what the Englishman really is.

When, after months of travel, one returns to England, one can taste, smell, and feel the difference in the atmosphere, physical and moral—the curious damp, blunt, good-humoured, happy-go-lucky, old-established slow-seeming formlessness of everything. You hail a porter; if you tell him you have plenty of time, he muddles your things amiably with an air of, "It'll be all right," till you have only just time. But if you tell him you have no time—he will set himself to catch that train for you, and catch it faster than a porter of any other country. Let no foreigner, however, experiment to prove the truth of this, for a porter—like any other Englishman—is incapable of taking a foreigner seriously, and, quite friendly, but a little pitying, will lose him the train, assuring the unfortunate that he can't possibly know what train he wants to catch.

The Englishman must have a thing brought under his nose before he will act; bring it there and he will go on acting after everybody else has stopped. He lives very much in the moment because he is essentially a man of facts and not a man of imagination. Want of imagination makes him, philosophically speaking, rather ludicrous; in practical affairs it handicaps him at the start; but once he has "got going"—as we say—it is of incalculable assistance to his stamina. The Englishman, partly through his lack of imagination and nervous sensibility, partly through his inbred dislike of extremes and habit of minimising the expression of everything, is a perfect example of the conservation of energy. It is, therefore, very difficult to come to the end of him. Add to this his unimaginative practicality, and tenacious moderation, his inherent spirit of competition—not to say pugnacity—a spirit of competition so extreme that it makes him, as it were, patronize Fate; add the sort of vulgarity that grows like fungus on people who despise ideas and analysis, and make a cult of unintellectuality; add a peculiar, ironic, "don't care" sort of humour; an underground humaneness, and an ashamed idealism—and you get some notion of the pudding of English character. It has a kind of terrible coolness, a rather awful level-headedness —by no means reflected in his Press. The Englishman makes constant small blunders; but few, almost no, deep mistakes. He is a slow starter, but there is no stronger finisher, because he has by temperament and training the faculty of getting through any job he gives his mind to with a minimum expenditure of vital energy; nothing is wasted in expression, style, spread-eagleism; everything is instinctively kept as near to the practical heart of the matter as possible. He is—to the eyes of an artist—distressingly matter-of-fact; a tempting mark for satire. And yet he is at bottom an idealist, though it is his nature to snub, disguise, and mock his own inherent optimism. To admit enthusiasm is "bad form" if he is a "gentleman"; and "swank," or mere waste of good heat, if he is not a "gentleman." England produces more than its proper percentage of cranks and poets; this is Nature's way of redressing the balance in a country where feelings are not shown, sentiments not expressed, and extremes laughed at. Not that the Englishman is cold, as is generally supposed in foreign countries—on the contrary he is warm-hearted and feels strongly; but just as peasants, for lack of words to express their feelings, become stolid, so does the Englishman, from sheer lack of the habit of self-expression. The Englishman's proverbial "hypocrisy"—that which I myself have dubbed his "island Pharisaism"—comes chiefly, I think, from his latent but fearfully strong instinct for competition which will not let him admit himself beaten, or in the wrong, even to himself; and from an ingrained sense of form that impels him always to "save his face"; but partly it comes from his powerlessness to explain his feelings. He has not the clear and fluent cynicism of expansive natures, wherewith to confess exactly how he stands.

It is the habit of men of all nations to want to have things both ways; the Englishman wants it both ways, I think, more strongly than any; and he is unfortunately so unable to express himself, *even to himself,* that he has never realized this truth, much less confessed it—hence his "hypocrisy."

He is sometimes abused for being over-attached to money. His island position, his early discoveries of coal, iron and processes of manufacture have made him, of course, a confirmed industrialist and trader; but he is more of an adventurer in wealth than a heaper-up of it. He is far from sitting on his money-bags—has no vein of proper avarice (the humble Englishman is probably the least provident man in the world)—and for national ends he will spill out his money like water, if convinced of the necessity.

In everything it comes to this with the Englishman —he must be convinced; and he takes a lot of convincing. He absorbs ideas slowly; would rather not imagine anything decidedly till he is obliged; but in proportion to the slowness with which he can be moved, is the slowness with which he can be removed! Hence the symbol of the bulldog. When he does see and seize a thing, he holds fast.

Because he has so little imagination, so little power of expression, he is saving nerve all the time. Because he never goes to extremes he is saving energy of body and spirit. The Englishman does not look into himself; he does not brood; he sees no further forward than is necessary; and he must have his joke. His is a fibre like rubber, that may be frayed and bent a little this way and that, but can neither be permeated nor broken.

1915.

FRANCE, 1916–1917

AN IMPRESSION

FRANCE, 1916-1917

I T was past eleven and the packet had been steady
some time when we went on deck and found her
moving slowly in bright moonlight up the haven
towards the houses of Le Havre. A night approach
to a city by water has the quality of other-worldness.
I remember the same sensation twice before: coming
in to San Francisco from the East by the steam-
ferry, and stealing into Abingdon-on-Thames in a
rowing-boat. Le Havre lay, reaching up towards the
heights, still and fair, a little mysterious, with many
lights which no one seemed using. It was cold, but
the air already had a different texture, drier, lighter
than the air we had left, and one's heart felt light
and a little excited. In the moonlight the piled-up,
shuttered houses had colouring like that of flowers
at night—pale, subtle, mother-o'-pearl. We moved
slowly up beside the quay, heard the first French
voices, saw the first French faces, and went down
again to sleep.

In the Military Bureau at the station, with what
friendly politeness they exchanged our hospital passes
for the necessary forms; but it took two officials ten
minutes of hard writing! And one thought: Is victory possible with all these forms? It is so throughout France—too many forms, too many people to

fill them up. As if France could not trust herself
without recording in spidery handwriting exactly
where she is, for nobody to look at afterwards. But
France *could* trust herself. A pity!

Our only fellow-traveller was not a soldier, but
had that indefinable look of connection with the war
wrapped round almost every one in France. A wide
land we passed, fallow under the November sky;
houses hidden among the square Normandy court-
yards of tall trees; not many people in the fields.

Paris is Paris, was, and ever shall be! Paris is not
France. If the Germans had taken Paris they would
have occupied the bodily heart, the centre of her
circulatory system; but the spirit of France their
hands would not have clutched, for it never dwelt
there. Paris is hard and hurried; France is not. Paris
loves pleasure; France loves life. Paris is a brilliant
stranger in her own land. And yet a lot of true
Frenchmen and Frenchwomen live there, and many
little plots of real French life are cultivated.

At the Gare de Lyon *poilus* are taking trains for
the South. This is our first real sight of them in their
tired glory. They look weary and dusty and strong;
every face has character, no face looks empty or as
if its thought were being done by others. Their
laughter is not vulgar or thick. Alongside their faces
the English face looks stupid, the English body
angular and—neat. They are loaded with queer bur-
dens, bread and bottles bulge their pockets; their
blue-grey is prettier than khaki, their round helmets
are becoming. Our Tommies, even to our own eyes,

seem uniformed, but hardly two out of all these poilus are dressed alike. The French soldier luxuriates in extremes; he can go to his death in white gloves and dandyism—he can glory in unshavenness and patches. The words *in extremis* seem dear to the French soldier; and, *con amore,* he passes from one extreme to the other. One of them stands gazing up at the board which gives the hours of starting and the destinations of the trains. His tired face is charming, and has a look that I cannot describe— lost, as it were, to all surroundings; a Welshman or a Highlander, but no pure Englishman, could look like that.

Our carriage has four French officers; they talk neither to us nor to each other; they sleep, sitting well back, hardly moving all night; one of them snores a little, but with a certain politeness. We leave them in the early morning and get down into the windy station at Valence. In pre-war days romance began there when one journeyed. A lovely word, and the gate of the South. Soon after Valence one used to wake and draw aside a corner of the curtain and look at the land in the first level sunlight; a strange land of plains, and far, yellowish hills, a land with a dry, shivering wind over it, and puffs of pink almond blossom. But now Valence was dark, for it was November, and raining. In the waiting-room were three tired soldiers trying to sleep, and one sitting up awake, shyly glad to share our cakes and journals. Then on through the wet morning by the little branch line into Dauphiné. Two officers again and a civilian, in our carriage, are talking in low voices of the war, or in higher voices of lodgings at Valence. One is a commandant, with a handsome paternal old face, broader than the English face, a little more in love with life, and a little more cynical about it, with more depth of colouring in eyes and cheeks and hair. The tone of their voices, talking of the war, is grave and secret. *"Les Anglais ne lacheront pas"* are the only words I plainly hear. The younger officer says: "And how would you punish?" The commandant's answer is inaudible, but by the twinkling of his eyes one knows it to be human and sagacious. The train winds on in the windy wet, through foothills and then young mountains, following up a swift-flowing river. The chief trees are bare Lombardy poplars. The chief little town is gathered round a sharp spur, with bare towers on its top. The colour everywhere is brownish-grey.

We have arrived. A tall, strong young soldier, all white teeth and smiles, hurries our luggage out, a car hurries us up in the rainy wind through the little town, down again across the river, up a long avenue of pines, and we are at our hospital.

Round the long table, at their dinner-hour, what a variety of type among the men! And yet a likeness, a sort of quickness and sensibility, common to them all. A few are a little *méfiant* of these new-comers, with the *méfiance* of individual character, not of class distrustfulness, nor of that defensive expressionlessness we cultivate in England. The French soldier has a touch of the child in him—if we leave out

the Parisians; a child who knows more than you do
perhaps; a child who has lived many lives before this
life; a wise child, who jumps to your moods and
shows you his "sore fingers" readily when he feels
that you want to see them. He has none of the per-
verse and grudging attitude towards his own ailments
that we English foster. He is perhaps a little inclined
to pet them, treating them with an odd mixture of
stoic gaiety and gloomy indulgence. It is like all the
rest of him; he feels everything so much quicker
than we do—he is so much more impressionable. The
variety of type is more marked physically than in
our country. Here is a tall Savoyard cavalryman,
with a maimed hand and a fair moustache brushed
up at the ends, big and strong, with grey eyes, and
a sort of sage self-reliance; only twenty-six, but
might be forty. Here is a real Latin, who was buried
by an explosion at Verdun; handsome, with dark
hair and a round head, and colour in his cheeks; an
ironical critic of everything, a Socialist, a mocker, a
fine, strong fellow with a clear brain, who attracts
women. Here are two peasants from the Central
South, both with bad sciatica, slower in look, with a
mournful, rather monkeyish expression in their eyes,
as if puzzled by their sufferings. Here is a true
Frenchman, a Territorial, from Roanne, riddled with
rheumatism, quick and gay, and suffering, touchy
and affectionate, not tall, brown-faced, brown-eyed,
rather fair, with clean jaw and features, and eyes
with a soul in them, looking a little up; forty-eight
—the oldest of them all—they call him *Grandpère*.

And here is a printer from Lyon with shell-shock;
medium-coloured, short and roundish and neat, full
of humanity and high standards and domestic affection, and so polite, with eyes a little like a dog's. And
here another with a shell-shock and brown-green
eyes, from the "invaded countries"; *méfiant,* truly,
this one, but with a heart when you get at it; neat,
and brooding, quick as a cat, nervous and wanting
his own way. But they are all so varied. If there are
qualities common to all they are impressionability
and capacity for affection. This is not the impression
left on one by a crowd of Englishmen. Behind the
politeness and civilised bearing of the French I used
to think there was a little of the tiger. In a sense
perhaps there is, but that is not the foundation of
their character—far from it! Underneath the tiger
again, there is a man civilised for centuries. Most
certainly the politeness of the French is no surface
quality, it is a polish welling up from a naturally
affectionate heart, a naturally quick apprehension of
the moods and feelings of others; it is the outcome
of a culture so old that, underneath all differences, it
binds together all those types and strains of blood—
the Savoyard, and the Southerner, the Latin of the
Centre, the man from the North, the Breton, the
Gascon, the Basque, the Auvergnat, even to some
extent the Norman and the Parisian—in a sort of
warm and bone-deep kinship. They have all, as it
were, sat for centuries under a wall with the afternoon sun warming them through and through, as I
so often saw the old town gossips sitting of an af-

ternoon. The sun of France has made them alike; a
light and happy sun, not too southern, but just southern enough!

And the women of France! If the men are bound
in that mysterious kinship, how much more so are
the women! What is it in the Frenchwoman which
makes her so utterly unique? A daughter in one of
Anatole France's books says to her mother: *"Tu es
pour les bijoux, je suis pour les dessous."* The
Frenchwoman spiritually is *pour les dessous.* There
is in her a kind of inherited, conservative, clever,
dainty capability; no matter where you go in France,
or in what class—country or town—you find it. She
cannot waste, she cannot spoil, she makes and shows
the best of everything. If I were asked for a concrete illustration of self-respect I should say—the
Frenchwoman. It is a particular kind of self-respect,
no doubt, very much limited to this world; and perhaps beginning to be a little frayed. We have some
Frenchwomen at the hospital, the servants who keep
us in running order—the dear cook whom we love
not only for her incomparable potato soup, proud of
her soldier son, once a professor, now a sergeant,
and she a woman of property, with two houses in
the little town; patient, kind, very stubborn about
her dishes, which have in them the essential juices
and savours which characterise all things really
French. She has great sweetness and self-containment in her small, wrinkled, yellowish face; always
quietly polite and grave, she bubbles deliciously at
any joke, and gives affection sagaciously to those

who merit. A jewel, who must be doing something *pour la France*. And we have Madame Jeanne Camille, mother of two daughters and one son too young to be a soldier. It was her eldest daughter who wanted to come and scrub in the hospital, but was refused because she was too pretty. And her mother came instead. A woman who did not need to come, and nearly fifty, but strong, as the French are strong, with good red blood, deep colouring, hair still black and handsome straight features. What a worker! A lover of talk, too, and of a joke when she has time. And Claire, of a *languissante* temperament, as she says; but who would know it. Eighteen, with a figure abundant as that of a woman of forty, but just beginning to fine down; holding herself as French girls learn to hold themselves so young; and with the pretty eyes of a Southern nymph, clear-brown and understanding, and a little bit wood-wild. Not self-conscious—like the English girl at that age—fond of work and play; with what is called "a good head" on her, and a warm heart. A real woman of France.

Then there is the "farmeress" at the home farm which gives the hospital its milk; a splendid, grey-eyed creature, doing the work of her husband who is at the front, with a little girl and boy rounder and rosier than anything you ever saw; and a small, one-eyed brother-in-law who drinks. My God, he drinks! Any day you go into the town to do hospital commissions you may see the hospital donkey-cart with the charming grey donkey outside the *Café de l'Univers* or what not, and know that Charles is within. He beguiles our *poilus,* and they take little beguiling. Wine is too plentiful in France. The sun in the wines of France quickens and cheers the blood in the veins of France. But the gift of wine is abused. One may see a poster which says—with what truth I know not—that drink has cost France more than the Franco-Prussian War. French drunkenness is not so sottish as our beer-and-whisky-fuddled variety, but it is not pleasant to see, and mars a fair land.

What a fair land! I never before grasped the charm of French colouring; the pinkish-yellow of the pantiled roofs, the lavender-grey or dim green of the shutters; the self-respecting shapes and flatness of the houses, unworried by wriggling ornamentation or lines coming up in order that they may go down again; the universal plane-trees with their variegated trunks and dancing lightness—nothing more charming than plane-trees in winter, their delicate twigs and little brown balls shaking against the clear pale skies, and in summer nothing more green and beautiful than their sun-flecked shade. Each country has its special genius of colouring— best displayed in winter. To characterise such genius by a word or two is hopeless; but one might say the genius of Spain is brown; of Ireland green; of England chalky blue-green; of Egypt shimmering sandstone. For France amethystine feebly expresses the sensation; the blend is subtle, stimulating, rarefied— at all events in the centre and south. Walk into an

71

English village, however beautiful—and many are
very beautiful—you will not get the peculiar sharp
spiritual sensation which will come on you entering
some little French village or town—the sensation one
has looking at a picture by Francesca. The blue
wood-smoke, the pinkish tiles, the grey shutters, the
grey-brown plane-trees, the pale blue sky, the yellowish houses, and above all the clean forms and the
clear air. I shall never forget one late afternoon rushing home in the car from some commission. The
setting sun had just broken through after a misty
day, the mountains were illumined with purple and
rose-madder, and snow-tipped against the blue sky,
a wonderful wistaria blue drifted smoke-like about
the valley; and the tall trees—poplars and cypresses
—stood like spires. No wonder the French are
spirituel, a word so different from our "spiritual,"
for that they are not; pre-eminently citizens of this
world—even the pious French. This is why on the
whole they make a better fist of social life than we
do, we misty islanders, only half-alive because we
set such store by our unrealised moralities. Not one
Englishman in ten now *really* believes that he is going to live again, but his disbelief has not yet rec-
onciled him to making the best of this life, or laid
ghosts of the beliefs he has outworn. Clear air and
sun, but not so much as to paralyse action, have made
in France clearer eyes, clearer brains, and touched
souls with a sane cynicism. The French do not
despise and neglect the means to ends. They face
sexual realities. They know that to live well they

72

must eat well, to eat well must cook well, to cook well must cleanly and cleverly cultivate their soil. May France be warned in time by our dismal fate! May she never lose her love of the land; nor let industrialism absorb her peasantry, and the lure of wealth and the cheap glamour of the towns draw her into their uncharmed circles. We English have rattled deep into a paradise of machines, chimneys, cinemas, and halfpenny papers; have bartered our heritage of health, dignity, and looks for wealth, and badly distributed wealth at that. France was trembling on the verge of the same precipice when the war came; with its death and wind of restlessness the war bids fair to tip her over. Let her hold back with all her might! Her two dangers are drink and the lure of the big towns. No race can preserve sanity and refinement which really gives way to these. She will not fare even as well as we have if she yields; our fibre is coarser and more resistant than hers, nor had we ever so much grace to lose. It is by grace and self-respect that France had her pre-eminence; let these wither, as wither they must in the grip of a sordid and drink-soothed industrialism, and her star will burn out. The life of the peasant is hard; peasants are soon wrinkled and weathered; they are not angels; narrow and over-provident, suspicious, and given to drink, yet they have their roots and being in the realities of life, close to nature, and keep a sort of simple dignity and health which great towns destroy. Let France take care of her peasants and her country will take care of itself.

Talking to our *poilus* we remarked that they have not a good word to throw to their *deputés*—no faith in them. About French politicians I know nothing; but their shoes are unenviable, and will become too tight for them after the war. The *poilu* has no faith at all now, if he ever had, save faith in his country, so engrained that he lets the life-loving blood of him be spilled out to the last drop, cursing himself and everything for his heroic folly.

We had a young Spaniard of the Foreign Legion in our hospital who had been to Cambridge, and had the "outside" eyes on all things French. In his view the French army has its thumb to its nose. Strange if it had not! Clear, quick brains cannot stand Fate's making ninepins of mankind year after year like this. Fortunately for France, the love of her sons has never been forced; it has grown like grass and simple wild herbs in the heart, alongside the liberty to criticise and blame. The *poilu* cares for nothing, no, not he! But he is himself a little, unconscious bit of France, and, for oneself, one always cares. State-forced patriotism made this war—a fever-germ which swells the head and causes blindness. A State which teaches patriotism in its schools is going mad! Let no such State be trusted! They who, after the war, would have England and France copy the example of the State-drilled country which opened these flood-gates of death, and teach mad provincialism under the nick-name of patriotism to their children, are driving nails into the coffins of their countries. Thumb to the nose is a natural product of three years

of war, and better by far than the docile despair to
which so many German soldiers have been reduced.
We were in Lyon when the Russian Revolution and
the German retreat from Bapaume were reported.
The town and railway station were full of soldiers.
No enthusiasm, no stir of any kind, only the usual
tired stoicism. And one thought of what the *poilu*
can be like; of our Christmas dinner-table at the
hospital under the green hanging wreaths and the
rosy Chinese lanterns, the hum, the chatter, the
laughter of free and easy souls in their red hospital
jackets. The French are so easily, so incorrigibly
gay, the dreary grinding pressure of this war seems
horribly cruel applied to such a people, and the hero-
ism with which they have borne its untold miseries
is sublime. In our little remote town out there—a
town which had been Roman in its time, and still
had bits of Roman walls and Roman arches—every
family had its fathers, brothers, sons, dead, fighting,
in prison or in hospital. The mothers were wonderful. One old couple, in a *ferblanterie* shop, who had
lost their eldest son and whose other son was at the
front, used to try hard not to talk about the war, but
sure enough they would come to it at last, each time
we saw them, and in a minute the mother would be
crying and a silent tear would roll down the old
father's face. Then he would point to the map and
say: "But look where they are, the Boches! Can we
stop? It's impossible. We must go on till we've
thrown them out. It is dreadful, but what would you
have? Ah! Our son—he was so promising!" And the

mother, weeping over the tin-tacks, would make the neatest little parcel of them, murmuring out of her tears: *"Il faut que ça finisse; mais la France—il ne faut pas que la France—Nos chers fils auraient été tués pour rien!"* Poor souls! I remember another couple up on the hillside. The old wife, dignified as a duchess—if duchesses are dignified—wanting us so badly to come in and sit down that she might the better talk to us of her sons: one dead, and one wounded, and two still at the front, and the youngest not yet old enough. And while we stood there up came the father, an old farmer, with that youngest son. He had not quite the spirit of the old lady, nor her serenity; he thought that men in these days were no better than *des bêtes féroces.* And in truth his philosophy—of an old tiller of the soil—was as superior to that of emperors and diplomats as his life is superior to theirs. Not very far from that little farm is the spot of all others in that mountain country which most stirs the æsthetic and the speculative strains within one. Lovely and remote, all by itself at the foot of a mountain, in a circle of the hills, an old monastery stands, now used as a farm, with one rose window, like a spider's web, spun delicate in stone tracery. There the old monks had gone to get away from the struggles of the main valley and the surges of the fighting men. There even now were traces of their peaceful life; the fish-ponds and the tillage still kept in cultivation. If they had lived in these days they would have been at the war, fighting or bearing stretchers, like the priests of France, of

whom eleven thousand, I am told—untruthfully, I
hope—are dead. So the world goes forward—the
Kingdom of Heaven comes!

We were in the town the day that the 1918 class
received their preliminary summons. Sad were the
mothers watching their boys parading the streets,
rosetted and singing to show that they had passed
and were ready to be food for cannon. Not one of
those boys, I daresay, in his heart wanted to go;
they have seen too many of their brethren return
war-worn, missed too many who will never come
back. But they were no less gay about it than those
recruits we saw in the spring of 1913, at Argèles in
the Pyrenees, singing along and shouting on the day
of their enrolment.

There were other reminders to us, and to the little
town, of the blood-red line drawn across the map of
France. We had in our hospital men from the invaded countries without news of wives and families
mured up behind that iron veil. Once in a way a tiny
word would get through to them, and anxiety would
lift a little from their hearts; for a day or two they
would smile. One we had, paralysed in the legs, who
would sit doing macramé work and playing chess all
day long; every relative he had—wife, father,
mother, sisters—all were in the power of the German. As brave a nature as one could see in a year's
march, touchingly grateful, touchingly cheerful, but
with the saddest eyes I ever saw. There was one
little reminder in the town whom we could never help
going in to look at whenever we passed the shop

whose people had given her refuge. A little girl of eight with the most charming, grave, pale, little, grey-eyed face; there she would sit, playing with her doll, watching the customers. That little refugee at all events was beloved and happy; only I think she thought we would kidnap her one day—we stared at her so hard. She had the quality which gives to certain faces the fascination belonging to rare works of art.

With all this poignant bereavement and long-suffering amongst them it would be odd indeed if the gay and critical French nature did not rebel, and seek some outlet in apathy or bitter criticism. The miracle is that they go on and on holding fast. Easily depressed, and as easily lifted up again, grumble they must and will; but their hearts are not really down to the pitch of their voices; their love of country, which with them is love of self—the deepest of all kinds of patriotism—is too absolute. These two virtues or vices (as you please)—critical faculty and *amour propre* or vanity, if you prefer it—are in perpetual encounter. The French are at once not at all proud of themselves and very proud. They destroy all things French, themselves included, with their brains and tongues, and exalt the same with their hearts and by their actions. To the reserved English mind, always on the defensive, they seem to give themselves away continually; but he who understands sees it to be all part of that perpetual interplay of opposites which makes up the French character and secures for it in effect a curious vibrating equilibrium. "Intensely alive" is the chief impression one has of the French. They balance between head and heart at top speed in a sort of electric and eternal see-saw. It is this perpetual quick change which gives them, it seems to me, their special grip on actuality; they never fly into the cloud-regions of theories and dreams; their heads have not time before their hearts have intervened, their hearts not time before their heads cry: "Hold!" They apprehend both worlds, but with such rapid alternation that they surrender to neither. Consider how clever and comparatively warm is that cold thing "religion" in France. I remember so well the old *curé* of our little town coming up to lunch, his interest in the cooking, in the practical matters of our life, and in wider affairs too; his enjoyment of his coffee and cigarette; and the curious suddenness with which something seemed "to come over him"—one could hear his heart saying: "O my people, here am I wasting my time; I must run to you." I saw him in the court-yard talking to one of our *poilus,* not about his soul, but about his body; stroking his shoulder softly and calling him *mon cher fils*—a dear old man! Even religion here does not pretend to more than it can achieve—help and consolation to the bewildered and the suffering. It uses forms, smiling a little at them.

The secret of French culture lies in this vibrating balance; from quick marriage of mind and heart, reason and sense, in the French nature, all the clear created forms of French life arise, forms recognised

79

as forms with definite utility attached. Controlled expression is the result of action and reaction. Controlled expression is the essence of culture, because it alone makes a sufficiently clear appeal in a world which is itself the result of the innumerable interplay of complementary or duel laws and forces. French culture is near to the real heart of things, because it has a sort of quick sanity which never loses its way; or, when it does, very rapidly recovers the middle of the road. It has the two capital defects of its virtues. It is too fond of forms and too mistrustful. The French nature is sane and cynical. Well, it's natural! The French lie just halfway between north and south; their blood is too mingled for enthusiasm, and their culture too old.

I never realised how old France was till we went to Arles. In our crowded train *poilus* were packed, standing in the corridors. One very weary, invited by a high and kindly colonel into our carriage, chatted in his tired voice of how wonderfully the women kept the work going on the farms. "When we get a fortnight's leave," he said, "all goes well, we can do the heavy things the women can't, and the land is made clean. It wants that fortnight now and then, *mon colonel;* there is work on farms that women cannot do." And the colonel vehemently nodded his thin face. We alighted in the dark among southern forms and voices, and the little hotel omnibus became enmeshed at once in old, high, very narrow, Italian-seeming streets. It was Sunday next day; sunny, with a clear blue sky. In the square before

our hotel a simple crowd round the statue of Mistral
chattered or listened to a girl singing excruciating
songs; a crowd as old-looking as in Italy or Spain,
aged as things only are in the South. We walked
up to the Arena. Quite a recent development in the
life of Arles, they say, that marvellous Roman building, here cut down, there built up, by Saracen hands.
For a thousand years or more before the Romans
came Arles flourished and was civilised. What had
we mushroom islanders before the Romans came?
What had barbaric Prussia? Not even the Romans
to look forward to! The age-long life of the South
stands for much in modern France, correcting the
cruder blood which has poured in these last fifteen
hundred years. As one blends wine of very old stock
with newer brands, so has France been blended and
mellowed. A strange cosmic feeling one had, on the
top of the great building in that town older than
Rome itself, of the continuity of human life and the
futility of human conceit. The provincial vanity of
modern States looked pitiful in the clear air above
that vast stony proof of age.

In many ways the war has brought us up all standing on the edge of an abyss. When it is over shall we
go galloping over the edge, or, reining back, sit
awhile in our saddles looking for a better track? We
were all on the highway to a hell of material ex-
pansion and vulgarity, of cheap immediate profit,
and momentary sensation; north and south in our
different ways, all "rattling into barbarity." Shall
we find our way again into a finer air, where self-

respect, not profit, rules, and rare things and durable are made once more?

From Arles we journeyed to Marseilles, to see how the first cosmopolitan town in the world fared in war-time. Here was an amazing spectacle of swarming life. If France has reason to feel the war most of all the great countries, Marseilles must surely feel it less than any other great town; she flourishes in a perfect riot of movement and colour. Here all the tribes are met, save those of Central Europe—Frenchman, Serb, Spaniard, Algerian, Greek, Arab, Khabyle, Russian, Indian, Italian, Englishman, Scotsman, Jew, and Nubian rub shoulders in the thronged streets. The miles of docks are crammed with ships. Food of all sorts abounds. In the bright, dry light all is gay and busy. The most æsthetic, and perhaps most humiliating, sight that a Westerner could see we came on there: two Arab Spahis walking down the main street in their long robe uniforms, white and red, and their white linen bonnets bound with a dark fur and canting slightly backwards. Over six feet high, they moved unhurrying, smoking their cigarettes, turning their necks slowly from side to side like camels of the desert. Their brown, thin, bearded faces wore neither scorn nor interest, only a superb self-containment; but, beside them, every other specimen of the human race seemed cheap and negligible. God knows of what they were thinking—as little probably as the smoke they blew through their chiselled nostrils—but their beauty and grace were unsurpassable. And, visioning our western and northern towns, and the little, white, worried, abortions they breed, one felt downcast and abashed.

Marseilles swarmed with soldiers; Lyon, Valence, Arles, even the smallest cities swarmed with soldiers, and this at the moment when the Allied offensive was just beginning. If France be nearing the end of her man power, as some assert, she conceals it so that one would think she was at the beginning.

From Marseilles we went to Lyon. I have heard that town described as lamentably plain; but compared with Manchester or Sheffield it is as heaven to hell. Between its two wide rolling rivers, under a line of heights, it has somewhat the aspect of an enormous commercialised Florence. Perhaps in foggy weather it may be dreary, but the sky was blue and the sun shone, a huge *Foire* was just opening and every street bustled in a dignified manner.

The English have always had a vague idea that France is an immoral country. To the eye of a mere visitor France is the most moral of the four Great Powers—France, Russia, England, Germany; has the strongest family life and the most seemly streets. Young men and maidens are never seen walking or lying about, half-embraced, as in puritanical England. Fire is not played with—openly, at least. The slow-fly amorousness of the British working classes evidently does not suit the quicker blood of France. There is just enough of the South in the French to keep demonstration of affection away from daylight. A certain school of French novelist, with high-coloured tales of Parisian life, is responsible for his country's reputation. Whatever the Frenchman about town may be, he seems by no means typical of the many millions of Frenchmen who are not about town. And if Frenchwomen, as I have heard Frenchmen say, are *légères,* they are the best mothers in the world, and their "lightness" is not vulgarly obtruded. They say many domestic tragedies will be played at the conclusion of the war. If so, they will not be played in France alone; and compared with the tragedies of fidelity played all these dreadful years they will be as black rabbits to brown for numbers. For the truth on morality in France we must go back, I suspect, to that general conclusion about the French character—the swift passage from head to heart and back again, which, prohibiting extremes of puritanism and of licence, preserves a sort of balance.

From this war France will emerge changed, though less changed very likely than any other country. A certain self-sufficiency that was very marked about French life will have sloughed away. I expect at least some opening of the doors, some toleration of other tastes and standards, a softening of the too narrow definiteness of French opinion.

Even Paris has opened her heart a little since the war; and the heart of Paris is close, hard, impatient of strangers. We noticed in our hospital that whenever we had a Parisian he introduced a different atmosphere, and led us a quiet or noisy dance. We had one whose name was Aimé, whose skin was like a baby's, who talked softly and fast, with little grunts, and before he left was quite the leading personality. We had another, a red-haired young one; when he was away on leave we hardly knew the hospital, it was so orderly. The sons of Paris are a breed apart, just as our Cockneys are. I do not pretend to fathom them; they have the texture and resilience of an indiarubber ball. And the women of Paris! Heaven forfend that I should say I know them! They are a sealed book. Still, even Parisians are less intolerant than in pre-war days of us dull English, perceiving in us, perhaps, a certain unexpected usefulness. And *à propos!* One hears it said that in the regions of our British armies certain natives believe we have come to stay. What an intensely comic notion! And what a lurid light it throws on history, on the mistrust engendered between nations, on the cynicism which human conduct has forced deep into human hearts. No! If a British Government could be imagined behaving in such a way, the British population would leave England, become French citizens, and help to turn out the damned intruders!

But *we* did not encounter anywhere that comic belief. In all this land of France, chockful of those odd creatures English men and women, we found only a wonderful and touching welcome. Not once during those long months of winter was an unfriendly word spoken in our hearing; not once were we treated with anything but true politeness and cordiality. *Poilus* and peasants, porters and officials, ladies, doctors, servants, shop-folk, were always considerate, always friendly, always desirous that we should feel at home. The very dogs gave us welcome! A little black half-Pomeranian came uninvited and made his home with us in our hospital; we called him Aristide. But on our walks with him we were liable to meet a posse of children who would exclaim, *"Pom-pom! Voilà Pom-pom!"* and lead him away. Before night fell he would be with us again, with a bit of string or ribbon, bitten through, dangling from his collar. His children bored him terribly. We left him in trust to our *poilus* on that sad afternoon when "Good-bye" must be said, all those friendly hands shaken for the last time, and the friendly faces left. Through the little town the car bore us, away along the valley between the poplar trees with the first flush of spring on their twigs, and the magpies flighting across the road to the riverbank.

The heart of France is deep within her breast; she wears it not upon her sleeve. But France opened her heart for once and let us see the gold.

And so we came forth from France of a rainy day, leaving half our hearts behind us.

1917.

SPECULATIONS

SPECULATIONS

W HEN we survey the world around, the wondrous things which there abound"—especially the developments of these last years—there must come to some of us a doubt whether this civilisation of ours is to have a future.

In Samuel Butler's imagined country, "Erewhon," the inhabitants had broken up all machinery, abandoned the use of money, and lived in a strange elysium of health and beauty. I often wonder how, without something of the sort, modern man is to be prevented from falling into the trombone he blows so loudly, from being destroyed by the very machines he has devised for his benefit. The problem before modern man is clearly that of becoming master, instead of slave, of his own civilisation. The history of the last hundred and fifty years, especially in England, is surely one long story of ceaseless banquet and acute indigestion. Certain Roman Emperors are popularly supposed to have taken drastic measures during their feasts to regain their appetites; we have not their "slim" wisdom; we do not mind going on eating when we have had too much.

I do not question the intentions of civilisation—they are most honourable. To be clean, warm, well nourished, healthy, decently leisured, and free to move quickly about the world, are certainly pure benefits. And these are presumably the prime objects of our toil and ingenuity, the ideals to be served, by the discovery of steam, electricity, modern industrial machinery, telephony, flying. If we attained those ideals, and stopped there—well and good. Alas! the amazing mechanical conquests of the age have crowded one on another so fast that we have never had time to digest their effects. Each as it came we hailed as an incalculable benefit to mankind, and so it was, or would have been, if we had not the appetites of cormorants and the digestive powers of elderly gentlemen. Our civilisation reminds us of the corpse in the Mark Twain story which, at its own funeral, got up and rode with the driver. It is watching itself being buried. We discover, and scatter discovery broadcast among a society uninstructed in the proper use of it. Consider the town-ridden, parasitic condition of Great Britain—*the country which cannot feed itself*. If we are beaten in this war, it will be because we have let our industrial system run away with us; because we became so sunk in machines and money-getting that we forgot our self-respect. No self-respecting nation would have let its food-growing capacity and its country life down to the extent that we have. If we are beaten— which God forbid—we shall deserve our fate. And why did our industrial system get such a mad grip on us? Because we did not master the riot of our inventions and discoveries. Remember the spinning jenny—whence came the whole system of Lancashire cotton factories which drained a countryside of peasants and caused a deterioration of physique from which as yet there has been no recovery. Here was an invention which was to effect a tremendous saving of labour and be of sweeping benefit to mankind. Exploited without knowledge, scruple, or humanity, it also caused untold misery and grievous national harm. Read, mark, and learn Mr. and Mrs. Hammond's book, *The Town Labourer*. The spinning jenny and similar inventions have been the forces which have dotted beautiful counties of England with the blackest and most ill-looking towns in the world, have changed the proportion of country- to town-dwellers from about three as against two in 1761 to two as against seven in 1911; have strangled our powers to feed ourselves, and so made us a temptation to our enemies and a danger to the whole world. We have made money by it; our standard of wealth has gone up. I remember having a long talk with a very old shepherd on the South Downs, whose youth and early married life were lived on eight shillings a week; and he was no exception. Nowadays our agricultural wage averages over thirty shillings, though it buys but little more than the eight. Still, the standard of wealth has superficially advanced, if that be any satisfaction. But have health, beauty, happiness among the great bulk of the population?

Consider the mastery of the air. To what use has it been put, so far? To practically none, save the destruction of life. About five years before the war some of us in England tried to initiate an international movement to ban the use of flying for military purposes. The effort was entirely abortive. The fact is, man never goes in front of events, always insists on disastrously buying his experience. And I am inclined to think we shall continue to advance backwards unless we intern our inventors till we have learned to run the inventions of the last century instead of letting them run us. Counsels of perfection, however, are never pursued. But what *can* we do? We can try to ban certain outside dangers internationally, such as submarines and aircraft, in war; and, inside, we might establish a Board of Scientific Control to ensure that no inventions are exploited under conditions obviously harmful.

Suppose, for instance, that the spinning jenny had come before such a Board, one imagines they might have said: "If you want to use this peculiar novelty, you must first satisfy us that your employees are going to work under conditions favourable to health" —in other words, the Factory Acts, Town Planning, and no Child Labour, from the start. Or, when rubber was first introduced: "You are bringing in this new and, we dare say, quite useful article. We shall, however, first send out and see the conditions under which you obtain it." Having seen, they would have added: "You will alter those conditions, and treat your native labour humanely, or we will ban your use of this article," to the grief and anger of those periwig-pated persons who write to the papers about grandmotherly legislation and sickly sentimentalism.

Seriously, the history of modern civilisation shows that, while we can only trust individualism to make discoveries, we cannot at all trust it to apply discovery without some sort of State check in the interests of health, beauty, and happiness. Officialdom is on all our nerves. But this is a very vital matter, and the suggestion of a Board of Scientific Control is not so fantastic as it seems. Certain results of inventions and discoveries cannot, of course, be foreseen, but able and impartial brains could foresee a good many and save mankind from the most rampant results of raw and unconsidered exploitation. The public is a child; and the child who suddenly discovers that there is such a thing as candy, if left alone, can only be relied on to make itself sick.

There is an expression—"high-brow"—maybe complimentary in origin, but become in some sort a term of contempt. A doubter of our general divinity is labelled "high-brow" at once, and his doubts drop like water off the public's back. Anyone who questions our triumphant progress is tabooed for a pedant. That will not alter the fact, I fear, that we are growing feverish, rushed, and complicated, and have multiplied conveniences to such an extent that we do nothing with them but scrape the surface of life. The underlying cause in every country is the increase of herd-life, based on machines, money-getting, and the dread of being dull. Everyone knows how fearfully strong that dread is. But to be capable of being dull is in itself a disease.

And most of modern life seems to be a process of creating disease, then finding a remedy which in its turn creates another disease, demanding fresh remedy, and so on. We pride ourselves, for example, on scientific sanitation; well, what is scientific sanitation if not one huge palliative of evils, which have arisen from herd-life, enabling herd-life to be intensified, so that we shall presently need even more scientific sanitation? The old shepherd on the South Downs had never come in contact with it, yet he was very old, very healthy, hardy, and contented. He had a sort of simple dignity, too, that we have most of us lost. The true elixirs *vitæ*—for there be two, I think—are open-air life and a proud pleasure in one's work; we have evolved a mode of existence in which it is comparatively rare to find these two conjoined. In old countries, such as Britain, the evils of herd-life are at present vastly more acute than in a new country such as America. On the other hand, the further one is from hell the faster one drives towards it, and machines are beginning to run along with America even more violently than with Europe.

We are, I believe, awakening to the dangers of this "Gadarening," this rushing down the high cliff into the sea, possessed and pursued by the devils of machinery. But if any man would see how little alarmed he really is—let him ask himself how much of his present mode of existence he is prepared to alter. Altering the modes of other people is delightful; one would have great hope of the future if we had nothing before us but that. The medieval Irishman, in Froude, indicted for burning down the cathedral at Armagh, together with the Archbishop, defended himself thus: "As for the cathedral, 'tis

94

true I burned it; but indeed an' I wouldn't have, only they told me himself was inside." We are all ready to alter our opponents, if not to burn them. But even if we were as ardent reformers as that Irishman we could hardly force men to live in the open, or take a proud pleasure in their work, or enjoy beauty, or not concentrate themselves on making money. No amount of legislation will make us "lilies of the field" or "birds of the air," or prevent us from worshipping false gods, or neglecting to reform ourselves.

I once wrote the unpopular sentence, "Democracy at present offers the spectacle of a man running down a road followed at a more and more respectful distance by his own soul." I am a democrat, or I should never have dared. For democracy, substitute, "Modern Civilisation," which prides itself on redress after the event, agility in getting out of the holes into which it has snouted, and eagerness to snout into fresh ones. It foresees nothing, and avoids less. It is purely empirical, if one may use such a "high-brow" word.

Politics are popularly supposed to govern the direction, and statesmen to be the guardian angels, of Civilisation. It seems to me that they have little or no power over its growth. They are of it, and move with it. Their concern is rather with the body than with the mind or soul of a nation. One needs not to be an engineer to know that to pull a man up a wall one must be higher than he; that to raise general taste one must have better taste than that of those whose taste he is raising.

95

Now, to my indifferent mind, education in the
large sense—not politics at all—is the only agent
really capable of improving the trend of civilization,
the only lever we can use. Believing this, I think it a
thousand pities that neither Britain nor America,
nor so far as I know, any other country, has as yet
evolved machinery through which there might be
elected a supreme Director—or, say, a little Board
of three Directors—of the nation's spirit, an Educational President, as it were, with power over the
nation's spirit analogous to that which America's
elected political President has over America's body.
Our Minister of Education is as a rule an ordinary
Member of the Government, an ordinary man of affairs—though at the moment an angel may have
strayed in. Why cannot education be regarded, like
religion in the past, as something sacred, not merely
a department of political administration? Ought we
not, for this most vital business of education, to be
ever on the watch for the highest mind and the finest
spirit of the day to guide us? To secure the appoint-
ment of such a man, or triumvirate, by democratic
means, would need a special sifting process of elec-
tion, which could never be too close and careful. One
might use for the purpose the actual body of teachers
in the country to elect delegates to select a jury to
choose finally the flower of the national flock. It
would be worth any amount of trouble to ensure that
we always had the best man or men. And when we
had them we should give them a mandate as real and
substantial as America now gives to her political

President. We should intend them not for mere lay administrators and continuers of custom, but for true fountain-heads and initiators of higher ideals of conduct, learning, manners, and taste; nor stint them of the means necessary to carry those ideals into effect. Hitherto, the supposed direction of ideals—in practice almost none—has been left to religion. But religion as a motive force is at once too personal, too lacking in unanimity, and too specialised to control the educational needs of a modern State; religion, as I understand it, is essentially emotional and individual; when it becomes practical and worldly it strays outside its true province and loses beneficence. Education as I want to see it would take over the control of social ethics, and learning, but make no attempt to usurp the emotional functions of religion. Let me give you an example: Those elixirs *vitæ*— open-air life and a proud pleasure in one's work— imagine those two principles drummed into the heads and hearts of all the little scholars of the age, by men and women who had been taught to believe them the truth. Would this not gradually have an incalculable effect on the trend of our civilisation. Would it not tend to create a demand for a simple and sane life; help to get us back to the land; produce reluctance to work at jobs in which no one can feel pride and pleasure, and so diminish the power of machines and of commercial exploitation? But teachers could only be inspired with such ideals by master spirits. And my plea is that we should give ourselves the chance of electing and making use of such master spirits. We all know from everyday life and business that the real, the only problem is to get the best men to run the show; when we get them the show runs well, when we don't there is nothing left but to pay the piper. The chief defect of modern civilisation based on democracy is the difficulty of getting best men quickly enough. Unless Democracy—government by the people—makes of itself Aristocracy—government by the best people—it is running steadily to seed. Democracy to be sound must utilise not only the ablest men of affairs, but the aristocracy of spirit. The really vital concern of such an elected Head of Education, himself the best man of all, would be the discovery and employment of other best men, best Heads of Schools and Colleges, whose chief concern in turn would be the discovery and employment of best subordinates. The better the teacher the better the ideals; quite obviously, the only hope of raising ideals is to raise the standard of those who teach, from top to toe of the educational machine. What we want, in short, is a sort of endless band—throwing up the finest spirit of the day till he forms a head or apex whence virtue runs swiftly down again into the people who elected him. This is the principle, as it seems to me, of the universe itself, whose symbol is neither circle nor spire, but circle and spire mysteriously combined.

Democracies must not be content to leave the ideals of health and beauty to artists and a leisured class; that is the way into a treeless, waterless desert. It has struck me forcibly that we English-speaking democracies are all right underneath and all wrong on the surface; our hearts are sound, but our skin is in a deplorable condition. Our taste, take it all round, is dreadful. For a petty illustration: Ragtime music. Judging by its popularity, one would think it must be a splendid discovery: yet it suggests little or nothing but the comic love-making of two darkies. We ride it to death; but its jigging, jogging, jumpy jingle refuses to die on us, and America's young and ours grow up in the tradition of its soul-forsaken sounds. Take another tiny illustration: The new dancing. Developed from cake-walk, to fox-trot, by way of tango. Precisely the same spiritual origin! And not exactly in the grand manner to one who, like myself, has loved and believed in dancing. Take the "snappy" side of journalism. In San Francisco a few years ago the Press snapped a certain writer and his wife, in their hotel, and the next day there appeared a photograph of two intensely wretched-looking beings stricken by limelight, under the headline: "Blank and wife enjoy freedom and gaiety in the air." Another writer told me that as he set foot on a car leaving a great city a young lady grabbed him by the coat-tail and cried: "Say, Mr. Asterisk, what are your views on a future life?" Not in the grand manner, all this; but, if you like, a sign of vitality and interest; a mere excrescence. But are not these excrescences symptoms of a fever lying within our modern civilisation, a febrility which is going to make achievement of great ends and great work more difficult? We Britons, as a breed, are admittedly stolid; we err as much on that score as Americans on the score of restlessness; yet we are both subject to these excrescences. There is something terribly infectious about vulgarity; and taste is on the down-grade following the tendencies of herd-life. It is not a process to be proud of.

Enough of Jeremiads, there is a bright side to our civilisation.

This modern febrility does not seem able to attack the real inner man. If there is a lamentable increase of vulgarity, superficiality, and restlessness in our epoch, there is also an inspiring development of certain qualities. Those who are watching human nature are pretty well aware of how, under the surface, unselfishness, ironic stoicism, and a warm humanity are growing. These are the great Town Virtues; the fine flowers of herd-life. A big price is being paid for them, but they are almost beyond price.

When you come to think, modern man is a very new and marvellous creature. Without quite realising it, we have evolved a fresh species of stoic, even more stoical, I suspect, than were the old Stoics. Modern man has cut loose from leading-strings; he stands on his own feet. His religion is to take what comes without flinching or complaint, as part of the day's work, which an unknowable God, Providence, Creative Principle, or whatever it shall be called, has appointed. Observation tells me that modern man at large, far from inclining towards the new, personal, elder-brotherly God of Mr. Wells, has turned his face the other way. He confronts life and death alone. By courage and kindness modern man exists, warmed by the glow of the great human fellowship. He has rediscovered the old Greek saying: "God is the helping of man by man"; has found out in his unselfconscious way that if he does not help himself, and help his fellows, he cannot reach that inner peace which satisfies. To do his bit, and to be kind! It is by that creed, rather than by any mysticism, that he finds the salvation of his soul. His religion is to be a common-or-garden hero, without thinking anything of it; for of a truth, this is the age of conduct.

After all, does not the only real spiritual warmth, not tinged by Pharisaism, egotism, or cowardice, come from the feeling of doing your work well and helping others; is not all the rest embroidery, luxury, pastime, pleasant sound and incense? Modern man, take him, in the large, does not believe in salvation to beat of drum; or that, by leaning up against another person, however idolised and mystical, he can gain support. He is a realist with too romantic a sense, perhaps, of the mystery which surrounds existence to pry into it. And, like modern civilisation itself, he is the creature of West and North, of atmospheres, climates, manners of life which foster neither inertia, reverence, nor mystic meditation. Essentially man of action, in ideal action he finds his only true comfort; and no attempts to discover for him new gods and symbols will divert him from the path made for him by the whole trend of his existence.

This modern world stands revealed, from beneath

its froth, frippery, and vulgar excrescences, sound at core—a world whose implicit motto is: "The good of all humanity." But the herd-life, which is its characteristic, brings many evils, has many dangers; and to preserve a sane mind in a healthy body is the riddle before us. Somehow we must free ourselves from the driving domination of machines and money-getting, not only for our own sakes but for that of all mankind.

This earth is made too subtly, of too multiple warp and woof, for prophecy. When he surveys the world around, the wondrous things which there abound, the prophet closes foolish lips. Besides, as the historian tells us: "Writers have that undeterminateness of spirit which commonly makes literary men of no use in the world." So I, for one, prophesy not. Still, we do know this: The world is wide and Nature bountiful enough for all, if we keep sane minds. The earth is fair and meant to be enjoyed, if we keep sane bodies. Who dare affront this world of beauty with mean views? There is no darkness but what the ape in us still makes, and in spite of all his monkey-tricks man is at heart further from the ape than man has yet been.

1917-18.

CASTLES IN SPAIN

AN ADDRESS

CASTLES IN SPAIN

OF what do we moderns dream? What are our castles in Spain?

This question crossed my mind in Seville cathedral, that stone fabric of man's greatest dream in the ages to which we have been accustomed to apply the word "dark." Travellers in Spain consulting their guide-books, read: "On the eighth day of July, in the year 1401, the Dean and Chapter of Seville assembled in the Court of the Elms and solemnly resolved: 'Let us build us a church so great that those who come after us may think us mad to have attempted it!' The church took one hundred and fifty years to build."

And in that glorious building, raised by five succeeding generations, one could not help wondering wherein lay the superiority of ourselves, Children of Light, over those old Sons of Darkness.

We too dream, no doubt—not always with a Freudian complex; and our dreams have results, such as the Great Dam at Assouan, the Roosevelt Dam in Arizona, the Woolworth Building, the Forth Bridge, the Power Works at Niagara, the Panama Canal (which took one-tenth of the time the Sons of Darkness lavished on Seville cathedral). But all these things were dreamed and fabricked out for immediate material benefit. The old builders of pyramids, mosques and churches built for no physical advantage in this life. They carved and wrought and slowly lifted stone on stone for remote and, as they thought, spiritual ends. We moderns mine and forge and mason-up our monuments to the immediate profit of our bodies. Incidentally they may give pleasure to the spirit, but we did not exactly build them for that purpose. Have we raised anything really great in stone or brick for a mere idea since Christopher Wren built St. Paul's Cathedral?

Sons of Darkness and Children of Light, both have worshipped a half-truth. The ancients built for to-morrow in another world, forgetting that all of us have a to-day in this. They spent riches and labour to save the souls of their hierarchy, but they kept their labourers so poor that they had no souls to save. They left astounding testimony to human genius and tenacity, but it never seems to have ruffled their consciousness that they fashioned the beautiful with slavery, misery, and blood.

We moderns pursue what we call Progress. All our stupendous achievements have this progressive notion at their back. Brooklyn Bridge may look beautiful in any light, and Sheffield chimney-stacks may look beautiful in the dark, but they were not put up for that reason, nor even because we thought we were thereby handing our Presidents or Prime Ministers the keys of heaven. Modern engineers may be lovers of beauty and men of imagination, but their prime mistresses are Science, Industry, and Trade. We think that if we make the wheels go round fast enough mankind is bound to rise on the wings of wealth. Look after the body, we say, and the spirit will look after itself. Whether we save a greater proportion of our bodies than the ancients did of souls is the question; but no such trifling doubt shakes our belief in Progress. Our modern castle in Spain is in one word: "Production."

Most men and women have an instinctive love of beauty, and some natural pride in the work of their brains and hands: but machinery divides us from the ancients; quietly, gradually, it has shifted the central point of man's philosophy. Before the industrial era set in, men used to make things by hand; they were in some sort artists, with at least the craftsman's pride in their work. Now they press buttons, turn wheels; don't make completed articles; work with monotony at the section of an article—so many hours of machine-driving a day, the total result of which is never a man's individual achievement. "Intelligent specialism," says a writer on Labour Policy, "is one thing. It consists in one man learning how to do one thing specially well. But the sort of specialising which consists in setting thousands of human beings during their whole working lives to such soul-destroying jobs as fixing the bristles into a hair-brush, pasting labels on jam-pots, or nearly any one of the varieties of machine-tending, is quite another thing. It is the utter negation of human nature."

The tendency of modern "Production" is to centre a man's interest not in his working day, but outside of it—at least, in the lower ranks of industry. The old artificers absorbed culture, such as it was, from their work. In these days culture, such as it is, is grafted on to the workman in his leisure, as antidote to wheel-driving. Hewers, delvers, drawers of water in the past never, perhaps, took interest in their work; and there are still many among us to-day to whom their work is of absorbing interest. But, on the whole, the change has put pride of quantity above pride of quality. In old days the good thing was often naturally supplied; nowadays it is more often artificially demanded.

No one objects to production sanely and coherently directed to fine purposes. But this Progress of ours, which is supposed to take care of our bodies, and of which machinery is the mistress—does it progress? We used to have the manor-house with half-a-dozen hovels in its support. Now we have twenty miles of handsome residences with a hundred and twenty miles of ugly back streets, reeking with smoke and redolent of dullness, dirt, and discontent. The proportions are still unchanged, and the purple patches of our great towns are too often as rouge on the cheeks and salve on the lips of a corpse. Is this really Progress?

True progress would mean levelling up and gradually extinguishing the disproportion between manor and hovel, residence and back street.

Let us fantastically conceive the civic authorities of London on the eighth day of July, in this year of grace, solemnly resolving: "We will remake of London a city so beautiful and sweet to dwell in, that those who come after us shall think us mad to have attempted it." It might well take five generations to remake of London a stainless city of Portland stone, full of baths and flowers and singing birds—not in cages. We should need a procession of civic authorities who steadily loved castles in Spain. For a civic body only lives about four years, and cannot bind its successor. I wonder if we have even begun to realise the difficulty of true progress in a democratic age. He who furnishes an antidote to the wasteful, shifting tendency of short immediate policies under a system of government by bodies elected for short terms, might be the greatest benefactor of the age. For find that antidote we must, or discover democracy to be fraudulent.

Again, are we not unfortunate in letting civic life be run by those who were born seeing two inches before their noses, and whose education, instead of increasing, has reduced those inches to one? It seems ungrateful to criticise the practical business man, whose stamina and energy make the more imaginative gasp. One owes him much, but one would like to owe him more. For does his vision as a rule extend beyond keeping pace with the present? And without vision—the people perish! Has not the word "visionary" come to have a slighting significance? And yet, unless we incorporate beauty in our scheme of life to-day, and teach the love of beauty to our children, the life of to-morrow and the children thereof must needs be as far from beauty as we are now. Isn't it, then, peculiar to set men to direct the education, housing, and amusements of their fellow-citizens, unless they have a love of beauty and some considerable knowledge of art? And have not the present generation of business men—with notable exceptions —a sort of indulgent contempt for art and beauty? A few years ago the Headmaster of a great Public School made use of these words: "I'm glad to see so many boys going in for art; it is an excellent hobby to pass the time *when you have nothing better to do!*" He had been teaching Greek for half a century; yet it was Greek to him that art has been the greatest factor in raising mankind from its old savage state. The contemplation of beautiful visions, emotions, thoughts, and dreams, expressed beautifully in words, stone, metal, paint, and music, has slowly, generation by generation, uplifted man and mollified his taste for "long pig"—as the South Sea Islander calls his edible enemy. Even the uplifting part of religion is but the beautiful expression of exalted feeling. The rest of religion (including the ceremony of eating "long pig") is only superstition. Think of the thousand wars fought in the name of superstition; the human sacrifices, the tortures of the Inquisition; the persecutions, intolerances, and narrow cruelties perpetrated even to this day! The teachings of Buddha, of Christ, of St. Francis d'Assisi were the expression of exalted feeling; simple, and touching the hearts of men, as all true beauty does. They have done an ennobling work. But who shall deny that they belong to the cult of beauty?

Trade—they say—has been a mollifying factor, an elevator in the human hotel. Yes, in so far as it opens up communications, and is the coach in which art and beauty ride; but *of itself*—it has no elevating influence.

Beauty, alone, in the largest sense of the word—the yearning for it, the contemplation of it—has civilised mankind. And no human being ever contributed to that process who thought he had "something better to do." And yet, we don't take beauty seriously. Immediate profit rules the roost in this Age of ours, and I leave it to the conscience of the Age to decide whether that is good. For every Age has a conscience; though it never comes to life till the Age is on its death-bed.

The mistake of all Ages, perhaps, has lain in keeping the knowledge and the love of beauty as a preserve for the few, the possession of a caste or clique. No great proportion of us are capable of creating or expressing beauty; but an immensely greater proportion of us are capable of appreciating it than have ever been given the chance of so doing. It should be our castle in Spain to clear our Age of that defect, and put beauty within the reach of all.

Machinery, of course, has come to stay; and though it may be true that engineers, authors, stone-cutters, artists, and many others still love beauty and take pride in their work, the great majority of us—label-pasters, wheel-drivers, stokers, clerks, shop-girls, bristle-fixers—are the slaves of modern machinery. For all such we must rely on grafted culture now; in other words, on education, rousing and fostering in the young that instinct for beauty which is in nearly all of us. For this, we have exceptional facilities nowadays. Besides teaching cooking and the fine art of being clean, we can bring an inkling of the other fine arts, architecture, literature, painting, music, of past and present, to children even in the humblest schools, we can teach children to appreciate the beauty of Nature, and give them some idea of taste. Revolution or evolution—we glibly talk of now one, now the other, but both are vain unless they mean demand for greater dignity of human life. What use in B despoiling A if B is going to use his spoils no better, perhaps worse, than A?

The word beauty is not here used in any precious sense. Its precious definitions are without number, or —value to speak of. No! It is here used to mean everything which promotes the true dignity of human life. For instance, to be "a good sport"—as they say—a man will shun that which lowers his dignity, dims his idea of his own quality; and his conception of his own quality derives obscurely from his sense of beauty. The dignity of human life demands, in fact, not only such desirable embroideries as pleasant sound, fine form, and lovely colour but health, strength, cleanliness, balance, joy in living, just conduct and kind conduct. A man who truly loves beauty hates to think that he enjoys it at the expense of starved and stunted human beings or suffering animals. Mere æstheticism can be cruel or pettifogging; but such is not the beauty which gleams on the heights in the sunrise—certainly not our castle in Spain.

Sentiment apart, the ideal of beauty is the best investment modern man can make; for nothing else—not even trade—will keep him from extirpating the human species. Science in the hands of engineers and chemists has developed destructive power which increase a hundredfold with each decade, while the reproductive powers and inclinations of the human being do not vary. Nothing in the world but the love of beauty in its broad sense stands between Man and the full and reckless exercise of his competitive appetites. The Great War was a little war compared with that which, through the development of scientific destruction, might be waged next time. There is, then, sheer necessity for investment in the ideal of beauty. No other security will give us interest on our money, and our money back. Unbalanced trade, science, industry give, indeed, a high momentary rate of interest, but only till the crash comes again and the world goes even more bankrupt than it is at present. The professor who invented a rocket which would visit the moon, find out all about it, and come back with the story, would have done more real good if he had taught a school full of children to see the beauty of—moonshine.

The next war will be fought from the air, and from under the sea, with explosives, gas, and the germs of disease. It may be over before it is declared. The final war necessary for the complete extirpation of mankind will be fought, perhaps, with atomic energy; and we shall have no occasion to examine the moon, for the earth will be as lifeless.

But it is sentiment which really makes the wheels go round, for not even "big business" rules our instincts and passions, and the question for modern man is: What shall we be sentimental about? Which is the fairer castle in Spain—quantity or quality—blind production or the dignity of human life?

What ideals have we at present? Happiness in a future life. If there be a future life for the individual, shall we find it repaying if we have not striven for quality in this; not had that kind and free and generous philosophy which belongs to the cult of beauty, and alone gives peace of mind? The pursuit of beauty includes, then, whatever may be true in the ideal of happiness in a future life. We have another current ideal: wealth or comfort in this life. But the cult of beauty contains all that is good in that; for it demands physical health and well-being, sane minds in sane bodies, which depend on a sufficiency of material comfort. The rest of the ideal of wealth is mere fat, sagging beyond the point of balance. Modern civilisation offers us, in fact, a compound between "happiness in a future life" and "material comfort in this," lip-serving the first, and stomach-serving the second. You get the keys of heaven from your bank, but not unless you have a good balance. Modern civilisation, on the whole, is camouflaged commercialism, wherein to do things well for the joy of doing them well is mere eccentricity. We even commercialise salvation—for so much virtue, so much salvation! *Quid pro quo!*

To give the devil its due, ours is the best Age men

ever lived in; we are all more comfortable and virtuous than we ever were; we have many new accomplishments, advertisements in green pastures, telephones in bedrooms, more newspapers than we want to read, and extremely punctilious diagnosis of maladies. A doctor examined a young lady the other day, and among his notes were these: "Not afraid of small rooms, ghosts, or thunderstorms—not made drunk by hearing Wagner; brown hair, artistic hands; had a craving for chocolate in 1918." The Age is most thorough and accomplished, but with a kind of deadly practicality. All for to-day, nothing for to-morrow! The future will never think us mad for attempting what we do attempt; we build no Seville cathedrals. We never get ahead of time. For instance, we have just let slip a chance to re-vitalise the country life of England. At demobilisation we might have put hundreds of thousands on the land, which needs them so very badly. And we have put in all not so many as the war took off the land. Life on the land means hard work and fewer cinemas; but it also means hearty stock for the next generation and the power of feeding ourselves on an island which the next war might completely isolate. A nation which never looks ahead is in for rude awakenings.

The pursuit of beauty as a national ideal, the building of that castle in Spain, requires, of course, foresight, long and patient labour, and steadfastness of ideal.

All literary men can tell people what they ought

not to be; that is—literature. But to tell them what they ought to do is—politics, and it would be mere impertinence for a literary man to suggest anything practical!

But let him, at least, make a few affirmations. He believes that modern man is a little further from being a mere animal than the men of the Dark Ages, however great the castles in Spain those men left for us to look upon; but he is sure that we are in far greater danger than ever they were of a swift decline. From that decline he is convinced that only the love and cult of beauty will save us.

By the love and cult of beauty he means: *a higher and wider conception of the dignity of human life;* the teaching of what beauty is, to all—not merely to the few; the cultivation of good-will, so that we wish and work and dream that not only ourselves but everybody may be healthy and happy; and, above all, the fostering of the habit of doing things and making things well, for the joy of the work and the pleasure of achievement, rather than for the gain they will bring us. With these as the rules—instead of, as now, the riders—the wheels of an insensate scientific industrialism, whose one idea is to make money and get ahead of other people, careless of direction toward heaven or hell, might conceivably be spoked. Our Age lacks an ideal expressed with sufficient concreteness to be like a vision beckoning. In these unsuperstitious days no other ideal seems worthy of us, or indeed possible to us, save beauty—or call it, if you will, the dignity of human life.

Writers sometimes urge the need for more spiritual beauty in our lives. I distrust the word spiritual. We must be able to smell, and see, hear, feel, and taste our ideal as well; must know by plain evidence that it is lifting human life, and is the heritage of all, not merely of the refined and leisured. The body and soul are one for the purpose of all real evolution, and regrettable is any term suggestive of divorce between them. The dignity of human life is an unmistakable and comprehensive phrase. Offence against it is the modern Satan. We can say "Retro, Satanas," by leaving, each of us, a tiny corner of the universe a little more dignified, lovely, and lovable than we found it.

Latest opinion—unless there is a later—assigns ten thousand years as the time during which what we know as civilisation has been at work. But ten thousand years is a considerable period of mollification, and one had rashly hoped that traditions of gentleness and fair-play had more strength among Western peoples than they have been proved to have since 1914; that mob feeling might have been less, instead of, as it seems, more potent. And yet, alongside of stupidity, savagery, greed, and mob violence, run an amazing individual patience, good humour, endurance, and heroism, which save a man from turning his back on himself and the world, with the words: "Cats and monkeys, monkeys and cats; all life is there!" Fear, after all, is at the back of nearly all savagery; and man must infallibly succumb to the infections of fear if there be not present in him that potent antidote—the sense of human dignity, which is but a love of and a belief in beauty. What applies to the individual applies to the civilisation of which he forms a part. Our civilisation, if it is to endure, must have a star on which to fix its eyes—something distant and magnetic to draw it on, something to strive towards, beyond the troubled and shifting needs and passions and prejudices of the moment. Those who wish to raise the dignity of human life should try to give civilisation that star, to equip the world with the only vision which can save it from spite and the crazy competitions which lead thereto. The past few years have been the result of the past few hundred years. The war was no spasmodic visitation, but the culmination of age-long competitions. The past few years have devoured many millions of grown men, more millions of little children—prevented their birth, killed them, or withered them for life. If modern individuals and modern nations pursue again these crazy competitions, without regard for the dignity of human life, we shall live to see ten millions perish for every million who perished in this war. We shall live to curse the day, when, at the end of so great a lesson, we were too practical and businesslike to take it to heart.

Facts must be faced, and ideals should be grounded in reality; for it is no use blinking the general nature of man, or thinking that Rome can be built in a day. But with all our prejudices and passions, and all our "business instinct," we have also the instinct for beauty, and a sense of what is dignified. On that we must build, if we wish to leave to those who come after us the foundations of a castle in Spain such as the world has not yet seen; to leave our successors in mood and heart to continue our work, so that one hundred and fifty years, perhaps, from now human life may really be dignified and beautiful, not just a breathless, grudging, visionless scramble from birth to death, of a night with no star alight.

1920.

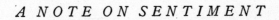
A NOTE ON SENTIMENT

A NOTE ON SENTIMENT

SENTIMENT (so far as literature is concerned) may be defined, I suppose, as the just verbal expression of genuine feeling; it becomes sentimentalism when the feeling is not genuine, or when the expression strikes the reader as laid on with too thick a pen. I find a good instance of the difference in a certain novel of my own, written at a time of stress, and re-read for the first time in calm days six years later. I found it sentimental, and started to revise it. By cutting out thirty thousand words, or just one-quarter of the book, without omitting or altering any of the incidents, or eliminating any of the characters, simply by chopping words out of almost every sentence and thereby removing the over-expression, I reduced the sentimentalism to sentiment, so far as I could judge.

In any definition of sentiment or sentimentalism, reader, in fact, as well as writer, is involved. That there is nothing absolute in the matter will be admitted even by holders of literary opinions canonised in coterie—nothing more absolute than in canonised opinion itself. Time plays skittles with the definitions of sentiment as freely as with the views of the criticaster. Not a Victorian novelist, English or American, save perhaps Marryat and Mark Twain, would escape being pilloried as sentimental by the sniffers of to-day. The cynic of 1870 is the sentimentalist of

1920. The sentimentalist of 1920 may become the cynic of 1970. Comparing Defoe, Fielding and Smollett with the Victorians, we see that the definition of sentiment follows the normal laws of reaction, or, perhaps more exactly, yields to the changes of education and environment. Young men or women of to-day, for example, with all their deep feelings, passions and sufferings still to come, and accustomed to the jibing prevalent where art is discussed but seldom achieved, will find almost any verbal expression of feeling "sentimental," while a farmer's wife, who would never in voice or vocabulary do ten per cent of justice to any emotion she might feel, will be approvingly stirred by a treacley situation in play or film, and shed tears over extravagantly false pathos in the books she reads. Nor can it be assumed that the more highly educated a person, the thinner the pen he demands of the writer who is expressing feeling. A Gilbert Murray may sometimes be moved by what a sucking poet would call "sentimental tosh!" In fact, there are all sorts of complications. There are readers, for instance, who hold that literature should not stir emotion in any way connected with life, but only rouse a kind of gloating sensation in the brain, and such readers—the equivalent of the old "æsthetes"—are highly vocal. There is the type of critic, with whom certain sorts of emotional expression, however thickly traced, escape the charge "sentimental" because connected with "the sportsman and the gentleman," but to whom certain other kinds are "slop" because not so well connected. There is the complication of the label. Label an author sentimental, and whatever he writes is sentimental, whether it really is or not. And, finally, every writer who expresses feeling at all has his own particular unconscious point of over-expression. Thomas Hardy, Joseph Conrad, even Bernard Shaw—not as a rule laid under this charge—can be sentimental in their own particular ways. The whole subject is intricate; nor is it helpful that what is sentimental to an Englishman is not sentimental to a Frenchman, and so forth.

Still, it may be laid down with some certainty that a writer must give adequate expression to his genuine feeling, or he will not be worth reading. And the whole matter lies in that word adequate. Let me cite four random examples of what I, at least, consider adequate verbal expression of true feeling: The poem called "The Bull," by Ralph Hodgson; the few pages describing the death of Bazarov in Turgenev's *Fathers and Children;* a story called "Life of Ma Parker," in Katherine Mansfield's volume *Bliss;* Thomas Hardy's little poem called "Afterwards," from the collection *Moments of Vision.* Adopting this test of *adequacy* the word sentimental, then, should only be applied where expression runs ahead of the writer's real feeling—in other words, in cases of insincerity, conscious or unconscious. The unconscious cases are, of course, the most common. Who does not know the auto-intoxications and hypnotisations by feeling, indulgence in which one's steadier sense afterwards repugns? But there is danger in too great readiness to pour cold water on the intoxications, whether of self or others. Juice and generosity in verbal expression are possibly more healthy than the under-expression of those afraid to give themselves away. There is a certain meanness in a dry and trained attitude of superiority to emotion, and in that slug-like temperament which prides itself on cold-bloodedness. English training is especially self-conscious. At root, perhaps a matter of climate; but in later stages, due to our public schools and universities, which strangely influence at second-hand classes not in direct touch with them. The guiding principle of English life and education is a stoicism discouraging all exhibition of emotion, and involving a high degree of self-control. For practical ends it has great value; for the expression and appreciation of art or literature, extremely little. It warps the critical point of view, removing it from an emotional to an ethical and practical basis. To indulge in emotional expression is bad for manners, for progress, trade, and will-power; and, freely using the word sentimental, we stamp on the habit. But art of any kind is based on emotion, and can only be duly apprehended through the emotional faculties. Letting these atrophy and adopting the posture of "sniff" we become deaf and dumb to art's true appeal. To "slop over" is the greatest offence an Englishman can commit. We hold it in such horror that our intellectuals often lose the power to judge what is or is not the adequate expression of feeling. But here again we have extraordinary contradictions. For alongside a considerable posture of "sniff" we have a multitude who wallow in the crudest sentimentalism, an audience for whom it is impossible to lay it on too thick.

Shifting to consideration of sentiment in practical affairs we shall find a state of things just as muddled. In the Law Courts for instance, a judge, out of a sentimental regard for marriage, will rebuke counsel for using the expression "this poor woman" of one who, having run away with her husband's brother, tries to atone by committing suicide. "She is a married woman," he says, and to pity her is sentimental. Or an advocate who will appeal in the most sentimental terms to the patriotism of a jury will stigmatise as "sentimental" appeals to feeling in cases of vivisection, wife-beating or other cruelties. Editors, statesmen, preachers, glaringly sentimental in expressing feelings which they think will tell on their audiences, in the same leading articles, speeches, or sermons will condemn the mawkish sentimentality of, say, conscientious objectors, with whose feelings it does not suit their case to agree. The rule in practical life seems to be that your own feeling is sound, and that of your adversary sentimental. The public man sentimentally attached to the idea of Empire or the idea of Progress proclaims the sentimentality of the little Englander or back-to-the-land-man, and honestly supposes himself as much without reproach of sentiment as he is without fear of serious retaliation, since he has behind him a vast bulk of similar sentimentalism. In fact, in life at large you may be sentimental without being called so only when you are on the side of the majority. One does not perhaps exaggerate in saying that we are all sentimentalists; and the difference between us is that most of us safely over-express popular sentiments, and a few of us riskily over-express sentiments which are not popular. Only the latter earn the title "Sentimentalists." Suppose a man to believe after sincere reflection that modern civilisation—with its riot of machinery, scientific experiment, exploitation of the air, and all the concomitant and ever-increasing desires and wants thereby roused in the human animal —has gone for the moment beyond the point of balance, beyond the rule *mens sana in corpore sano;* suppose he seriously considers that under this ever-multiplying taxation on nerve energy and time, under hypnotisation by a blind Progress, men are steadily losing hold on beauty, health, and goodness; that, in fact, his discoveries are being too much for his very moderate digestion, and that he ought for a time to call a halt—just as the individual who is living too fast must take a rest-cure or fall into his trombone—suppose, I say, that a man sincerely believes all this, will he escape being called a sentimentalist? Certainly not, for he is running counter to a sentimentalism much more popular than his own, a sentimentalism which believes in Progress (with a definition of what Progress is left out), talks of the indomitable human spirit, *per ardua ad astra,* and damns the consequences. If he says "More simplicity, fewer wants, home-grown food, not so much rushing about, more true beauty, more time to en-

joy it, better instruction in how to enjoy it"—in
other words, a normal temperature instead of 102—
he is a poor thing in the eyes of those who outnumber him a hundred to one. The point is this: he may
be wrong, but he is no more sentimental than they
are. And the moral of this and many another possible illustration is: "Before I call a man a sentimentalist, let me look well at myself, at my own feelings
and beliefs. I live in a very glass house; I must be
careful how I throw stones!"

Sentimentalism, then, whether in life or in literature, is simply a riding before the hounds. Of this
we are all guilty at times. But as often as not the
charge "sentimentalist" is a mere partisan term of
abuse, unfounded in fact; for it is not sentimental to
have strong feelings (however eccentric) and to give
them adequate, that is to say strong and sincere, expression.

But putting sentimentalism—over-expression—
aside, how far is it good that we should be men and
women of sentiment—moved, that is, by feeling
rather than by calculation, by the heart rather than
by the head? Again comes in the question of balance. Amongst people like the English—although a
most baffling and contradictory race—one would say
that, on the whole, the head predominates. What has
been called Anglo-Saxon phlegm or English common-sense rules the roost. For the stability of national life that is probably a blessing. If our judges,
our statesmen, our juries were men of feeling, it
might not work to our advantage, however much

their hard-headedness may annoy us at times. But the mere fact that one may nearly always rely in England on a majority of the common-sensical makes the man or woman of sentiment necessary and valuable among us. And one thing is clear: no amount of trying to be men of feeling can make us into them; we are, or we are not. The ideal, no doubt, is to have heart and head about equally developed— but the ideal is rare, as a search for instances will soon reveal.

1922.

SIX NOVELISTS IN PROFILE
AN ADDRESS

M Y first profile is that of Charles Dickens, who, born in London in 1812, died at Gadshill in 1870. In that early and in some sort great Victorian Age, English novelists—in spite of much generous revolt against particular social evils —solemnly accepted the conventions, morals, standards, ideals, and enterprises of their day; believed with all their hearts that life was worth living; regarded its current values as absolute; had no ironic misgivings, nor any sense that existence is a tragicomedy. They saw no grin on the face of Fate. They were almost majestically unself-conscious. Dickens was a true child of his age. Shakespeare, two hundred and fifty years earlier, was much more introspective and philosophical.

Dickens was an extraordinarily artless writer, he let his genius run where and when it would; the perfect master of happy extravagance; a natural stylist of extraordinary force, he was a born teller of a tale, with amazing knowledge of human nature and human types; a great imaginative creator, with the zest of a schoolboy at a Christmas feast.

He was an enemy of "humbug," fiercely resentful of cruelty, intolerance, and solemn stupidity, and his writing life was a long attack on the social evils he came across. He lashed officialism, hypocrisy, and the abuse of power. But in spite of this disposition to-wards satire, he makes us think always first of the story and the characters. All his spontaneous, crude, richly creative work is coloured with an eager, broad humanity. "All kind things," he once said, "must be done on their own account, and for their own sake, and without the least reference to gratitude."

Probably Dickens, like most novelists, accounted himself a poet. But there is little evidence to support this accusation. There was in him, moreover, no pa-ganism, no influence by Greek or Latin culture; no trace of any foreign influence; he was English of the English, and from no other writings can England be so well comprehended even now. If some of his char-acters were little more than names attached to ex-travagant attitudes of conduct, they show his genius the more in that we accept them as men and women. He had the persuasiveness of great vitality; he wrote with a fine "gusto." In the pages of Dickens virtue is virtue, vice vice, and seldom "the twain do meet" in the way they meet in all—except our public men. He paints the ethical with a glaring brush; we should charge at the picture as bulls at red if there were any pretence of art about it. But in those days our novel-ists did not bother about art. The literary gatherings of that period in England confined themselves, I sus-pect, to jesting, drink, politics, and oysters. Dickens' great contemporary, Thackeray, indeed, had heard of art, and thought it worthy of a certain patronage; Dickens himself identified it, I fear, with foreign-ers, and showed it the back door. He was robust, but it is strange to think of him writing as he did when, not two hundred miles away, such an accomplished artist as Prosper Merimée was writing *Carmen* and *The Venus d'Ille,* Turgenev was writing *Smoke* and *Torrents of Spring,* and across the Atlantic Nathaniel Hawthorne *The Scarlet Letter* and Edgar Poe his *Strange Tales.* No one would dream of going to Dickens to learn consciously the art of novel-writing; yet all can draw from him subconsciously the foundation of phrase, for he was a born writer, and the foundation of philosophy, though he was no philosopher.

Beyond dispute, he is, to me, the greatest English novelist, and the greatest example in the annals of all novel-writing of the triumph of sheer exuberant genius. By native imagination and force of expression he has left human nature imprinted on men's minds more variously and vividly than any other Western novelist.

Culture does not teach one to write novels.

Education in the technical sense serves rather to choke than to encourage the power of imagination. Before I began to write novels I had forgotten nearly all I learned at school and college. Precise scholars are rarely imaginative writers of any force, they know too much and too little. The vividly imaginative seldom have relish for the exact study of anything except—life. Feeling for the colour and rhythm of words may be helped by reading poetry and fine prose, but it is due more to inborn sensibility and a musical ear. The power of construction also is inborn. The power of poignant expression is inborn; it cannot be acquired, it can only be improved. Nor can anyone teach an imaginative writer to feel or see life in any particular way. After he has learned to read and write, a novelist can be taught by others only how *not* to write; his true schoolmaster is life itself.

Now, when, as we are all fond of doing, we use the word art in relation to the novel, we have to remember the novel's history; the variety of forms through which it has passed and is still passing since Cervantes and that first great Western novel, *Don Quixote*.

The early novels of all Western countries took a picaresque form; they were strings of biographical incident loosely joined by the thread of one or more central figures, rather like a string of onions and often with something of their savour. Unity and proportion, except of this crude nature, were not thought of. The novel had length but neither breadth nor roundness. Towards the beginning of the nineteenth century, one can see the novel growing rounder and rounder until, when Dickens wrote, the egg was, roughly speaking, its recognised shape—plethoric in the middle and skimpy at both ends, like a successful novelist. What conditioned this gradual change I cannot say, but the development was rather like that which we observe in painting at the time of the Renaissance. Under Jane Austen, Dickens, Balzac, Stendhal, Scott, Dumas, Thackeray and Hugo, the novel attained a certain relation of part to whole;

but it was left for one of more poetic feeling and greater sensibility than any of these to perfect its proportions, and introduce the principle of selection, until there was that complete relation of part to whole which goes to the making of what we call a work of art. This writer was Turgenev, as supreme in the art of the novel as Dickens was artless.

Ivan Turgenev, born at Orel in Russia in 1818, died at Bougival near Paris in 1883. Critics have usually been preoccupied by his detachment from his native Russian culture, by his variation from the loose-jointed giant Gogol, and the shapeless giant Dostoievsky. Anxiously calling him a Westerner, they have omitted to notice that the West did not influence him so much as he influenced the West. Turgenev achieved his unique position from within himself; he was the finest natural poet who ever wrote novels. It was *that* which separated him from his great Russian contemporaries, and gave him his distinction and his influence in the West. Russia did not like Turgenev—he had a bad habit: he told the truth. No country likes that. It is considered especially improper in novelists. Russia got rid of him. But if he had never left Russia his work would still have taken the shape it did—because of his instinctive feeling for form. He had a perfect sense of "line"; moulding and rounding his themes within himself before working them out in written words; and, though he never neglected the objective, he thought in terms of atmosphere rather than in terms of fact. Turgenev, an aristocrat, a man of culture, susceptible to the impression of foreign literatures, devoted to music and painting, a reader and writer of plays and poems, touches Dickens only at three broad but all-important points : the intense understanding they both had of human nature, the intense interest they both took in life, the intense hatred they both felt for cruelty and humbug. Let those who doubt the truth of this last resemblance read Turgenev's little story, *Mumu,* about the dog of the dumb serf porter Gerasim. No more stirring protest against tyrannical cruelty was ever penned in terms of art. Dickens was the least fastidious of writers, Turgenev one of the most fastidious. Dickens attacked a cruelty, an abuse, an extravagance, directly or by way of frank caricature; Turgenev sank his criticism in objective terms of portraiture. His style in Russian, we are told, is exquisite ; even in translations much of its charm and essential flavour lingers. His dialogue is easy, interesting, life-like, yet always significant and revealing ; his characters serve the main theme or idea with which he is dealing, but never fail to be real men and women too. His descriptions of Nature are delightful. *Byezhin Prairie, A Tryst, Torrents of Spring* haunt one with their beauty. The whole of his work is saturated in the half-melancholy rapture which Nature stirs in a poetic temperament. In his definite prose-poems he was much less of a poet than in his sketches and novels, because self-consciousness destroys true poetry, which is the springing forth of mood and feeling almost in spite of self. In Turgenev there is a slight survival of burlesque, a dash of the grotesque, a suspicion of what we should call "the old-fashioned"; but considering that he was in his prime sixty years ago, how marvellously little the machine of his art creaks!

The English novel, though on the whole perhaps more varied and rich than that of any other country, has—from *Clarissa Harlowe* down to *Ulysses*—been inclined to self-indulgence; it often goes to bed drunk. And it owes to Turgenev more than to any-one what niceness of deportment and proportion it now has. I, at least, acknowledge a great debt. To him and to de Maupassant I served that spiritual and technical apprenticeship which every young writer serves, guided by some deep kinship in spirit to one or other of the old past-masters of his craft. Flau-bert, the apostle of self-conscious artistry, never had quite the vital influence that Turgenev exercised on English writers; a certain feeling of enclosure clings about his work, an indoor atmosphere. Against Turgenev that was never charged, not even when, about the year 1907, it became a literary fashion in England to disparage him, because certain of our critics had discovered—rather late, perhaps—a new Russian lamp in Dostoievsky. There was room, one might have thought, for the two lights; but in the literary world it is difficult to light a new lamp with-out putting out an old one. That is now ancient his-tory, and Turgenev has recovered his name, but not his influence. He is too balanced, and too essentially poetic, for the new age.

And so I come to my third profile—that of one

who, I am told by some, is still read in his native France, and who, I am told by others, has been laid on the shelf. The great literary achievements of Guy de Maupassant, born in 1850 and dying in 1893, were crowded into a space of but twelve years. His name is popularly associated with the short story, but his full measure, to my thinking, can only be taken through his novels, and tales of medium length like *Boule de Suif* and *Yvette*. All his work, long or short, tragic or trivial, is dramatic in essence; and, though he wrote but little for the theatre, he was richly endowed with the qualities that make a great dramatist. In the essentials of style, he is the prince of teachers. The vigour of his vision, and his thought, the economy and clarity of the expression in which he clothed them, have not yet been surpassed. Better than any other writer, he has taught us what to leave out; better than any illustrated for us Flaubert's maxim: "Study an object till its essential difference from every other is perceived and can be rendered in words." His work forms a standing rebuke to the confusion, the shallow expressionism, the formless egoism which are not infrequently taken for art. But though disciplined to the finger-nails as a craftsman, he reached and displayed the depths of human feeling. His sardonic nature hated prejudice and stupidity, had in it a vein of deep and indignant pity, a burning curiosity, piercing vision, and a sensitiveness seldom equalled. He was well equipped for the rendering of life.

At times he wrote stories unworthy of him. At times his work smelled of the lamp. And the mental breakdown which clouded the end of his life left a searing mark on some of his later tales. But in spite of these defects, I follow the dictum of Tolstoi in placing Maupassant above his master Flaubert, both in style and temperamental gifts.

In Maupassant we reach, as it were, the apex of the shaped story, the high mark of fiction which knows exactly what it is about, and has for aim, through the objective method, revelation of the strange depths and shallows of human nature. A form of art highly disciplined and detached where the temperament of the author is allowed freedom only in the range of subject and character selected. In England Maupassant was once looked on as a ferocious realist; to literary youth he is now a rosy-fingered, pinafored romanticist, and his form considered too set, finished, and dramatic. Forgive, then, this quotation from his preface to *Pierre et Jean:*

"En somme, le public est composé de groupes nombreux qui nous crient : 'Consolez-moi.' 'Amusez-moi.' 'Attristez-moi.' 'Attendrissez-moi.' 'Faites-moi rêver.' 'Faites-moi rire.' 'Faites-moi frémir.' 'Faites-moi pleurer.' 'Faites-moi penser.' Seuls, quelques esprits d'élite demandent à l'artiste : Faites-moi quelque chose de beau, dans la forme qui vous conviendra le mieux, suivant votre tempérament. L'artiste essaie, réussit ou échoue."

His ideal was to make a fine or beautiful thing following his temperament. Since endless contro-

versy rages over the word "beauty," I shall be forgiven for not plunging into it. But the artist who
creates what is living and true has achieved beauty
also, in my considered opinion. De Maupassant made
many a capture of the shy bird Beauty.

It is curious to think that Tolstoi, whose profile is
so different, admired him. Born in 1828 at Yasnaya
Polyana in Russia, and dying in 1910 at Astaporo,
Leo Tolstoi began to write when he was twenty-
four years old, after a full and energetic youth.
Tales of Sevastopol, written during the Crimean
War, in which he served in the Russian army,
brought him instant celebrity. His chief masterpieces, *War and Peace* and *Anna Karenina,* were
written between 1864 and 1873.

Tolstoi is a fascinating puzzle. So singular an instance of artist and reformer rolled into one frame
is not, I think, elsewhere to be found. The preacher
in him, who took such charge of his later years, was
already casting a shadow over the artist-writer of
Anna Karenina. There is even an indication of the
moralist in the last part of that tremendous novel
War and Peace.

About his work, in fact, is an ever-present sense
of spiritual duality. It is a battlefield on which we
watch the ebb and flow of unending conflict, the
throb and stress of a gigantic disharmony. Explanation of this mysterious duality must be left to the
doctors now that our personalities are controlled by
our glands; so that if we have plenty of pituitary,
we are artists; and too little adrenal, perhaps, moralists.

In choosing a single novel to label with those words so dear to the confectioners of symposiums— "the greatest ever written"—I would select *War and Peace*. In it Tolstoi rides two themes, like a circus rider on his two piebald horses, and by a miracle reaches the stable door still mounted and still whole. The secret of his triumph lies in the sheer interest with which his creative energy has invested every passage. The book is six times as long as an ordinary novel, but it never flags, never wearies the reader, and prodigious is the amount of human interest and historical event, of social life and national life contained in it.

Tolstoi's method, in this novel as in all his work, is cumulative—the method of an infinity of fact and pictorial detail; the opposite of Turgenev's, who relied on selection and concentration, on atmosphere, and poetic balance. Tolstoi fills in all the spaces, and leaves little to the imagination; but with such vigour, such freshness, that it is all interesting. His "style" in the narrow sense is by no means remarkable; all his work bears the impress of a mind more concerned with the thing said than with the way in which to say it.

But if one may add to innumerable definitions: Style is the power in a writer to remove all barriers between himself and his reader—the triumph of style is the creation of intimacy. Then, though such a definition puts many stylists out of court, it leaves Tolstoi a stylist of mark, for no author, in his storytelling, produces a more intimate feeling of actual life. He is free, in fact, from the literary self-consciousness which so often spoils the work of polished writers. Tolstoi was carried away by his impulses, whether creative or reformative. He never stood on the shores of streams trying first one foot and then the other—that pet vice of modern art. Art, when it has life and meaning, comes from an artist possessed by his theme. The rest of art is just exercise in technique, which helps artists to render the greater impulses when they come—too seldom. The painter who spends half his life agonising over what he ought to be—Post-Impressionist, Cubist, Futurist, Expressionist, Dadaist, paulo-post-Dadaist, or whatever they are by now—who is ever developing a new and wonderful technique and changing his æsthetic outlook, does work which, like his mood, is self-conscious and tentative. But when a theme seizes on him all doubts about expression are resolved, and a master's work is wrought.

Tolstoi knew his Russian land and the Russian peasant as well, perhaps, as an aristocrat could know them; but he is not so close to the soul and body of Russia as Tchehov, who came of the people, and knew them from inside. The Russia of Tolstoi's great novels, *War and Peace* and *Anna Karenina,* is now a Russia of the past, perhaps only the crust of that Russia of the past—split and crumbled beyond repair. We are fortunate to have those two great pictures of a vanished fabric.

I pass to my fifth profile—that of Conrad.

Joseph Conrad Korzeniowski, born in 1857 of

are permitted to indulge in crude or violent feelings; the human intellect is the hub round which their scheme of things revolves. Conrad lived imaginatively in a world from which nothing was excluded, not even savagery, and where elemental nature, with its thoroughly bad manners, generally formed one if not two of the party.

The fascination of his writing lies in a singular blending of reality with romance—he paints a world of strange skies and seas, rivers, forests, men, strange harbours and ships, all, to our tamed understanding, touched a little by the marvellous. Beyond all modern writers he had lived romance; lived it for many years with a full unconscious pulse, the zest of a young man loving adventure, and before ever he thought to become a writer. How many talents among us are spoiled by having no store of experience and feeling, *unconsciously* amassed, to feed on! How many writers, without cream inside the churn, are turning out butter!

To peoples who have the sea in their blood, like the English, the appeal of Conrad is the greater. With the exception of Herman Melville in *The White Whale,* and Pierre Loti in *Pêcheurs d'Islande,* no novelist has so rendered the moods, the fascination, the menace of the sea. His writing of it is touched with awe and coloured by the inexhaustible interest of a man who has fought with and overcome or yielded to its infinite variety. *The Nigger of the 'Narcissus,' Typhoon,* and *Youth* are masterpieces indeed.

147

Passing from Conrad to the last of my profiles is to turn from Malay shores to the Quai d'Orléans. In life's drama Conrad was on the stage, Anatole France, from his birth in 1844 to his death in 1924, sat in the stalls. His was the detached and learned mind. A pure bookman, bred and born in the centre of bookish knowledge, he was erudite as few men have been, and withal—a scourge. His whip was the most elegant and perhaps the most effective ever wielded. He destroyed with a suavity that has never been excelled. He perforated prejudice and punctured idolatry so adroitly that the ventilation holes were scarcely visible, and the victims felt draughts without knowing why. In his long writing career— he began in 1868 and was still writing at his death in 1924—he only thrice, if I am not mistaken, assumed the rôle of novelist pure. *Le Crime de Sylvestre Bonnard, Le Lys Rouge* and *L'Histoire Comique* stand out in method from his other work. In them alone is he chiefly student of human character and teller of a tale. In his other books he is first the philosopher and satirist. Even a work of art so remarkable as *Thaïs,* a perfect piece of recreation, is in essence critical, and was forged out of a satiric heart. The Bergeret series, though they contain many admirable portraits, was the work of one preoccupied with riddling the prejudices rather than painting the features of human beings. The short masterpiece *Le Procurateur de Judée* presents an unforgettable effigy of Pontius Pilate, but it was written to clothe in perfection a satiric thought. Poor

"Crainquebille" is a very human figure, yet it is rather as a walking indictment of human justice that we cherish and remember him. Even little dog Riquet conveys his tail-fluttering criticism of human habits. Anatole France was a subtle and deadly fencer, rather than a trenchant swordsman like Voltaire; his victims still don't know that they are dead. They read him yet, and call him *maître*. Unsurpassed for lucidity and supple elegance, his style was the poetry of pure reason. He was very French. We shall never perhaps see again so perfect an incarnation of the witty French spirit. Not without justification did he take the *nom de plume* of France. His—like all the others in this little gallery—was the profile of a humanist, the most convinced and proselytising of them all. Born fortunately too late for the glory of being burned or beheaded, he succeeded in being excommunicated by the Vatican. Whether the pity which informed the greater part of his writings was the pity of feeling or of reason must be left to those who knew him personally; the urbanity and craft of its expression inclines one who did not know him to suspect the latter. His love, too, of wrapping his indictments in delicate robes of embroidered allegory has to some extent preserved him from attack by those whose creed is: "Say nothing that means anything, and be long about it." Excommunication by fashion is a glory he has not yet entirely achieved, though in certain Parisian coteries, and among the weaker-minded in New York, to admire him would be risky. One may say with certainty that he recoiled

from cruelty, narrowness, excess, and crudity—
Monsieur Bergeret was his spirit without its sting,
an intensely civilised being, incapable of life outside the ring of culture, Anatole France in the Malay seas, in the fields of Russia, in the purlieus of
Victorian London, among Normandy peasants, is—
unthinkable. He excelled in the ironic mingling of
values. *Le Jongleur de Notre Dame*—how tender his
irony could be! Loving the pagan, he yet seems to
have reverenced the heart of the Sermon on the
Mount, for *Heureux les Simples* is the moral of
many of his tales. His villagers might set up the
Virgin in gold and in ivory—but she ever fell down
till they set her up in plain wood. He revelled in
shredding away from the core of Christianity with
his thin chased knife all pretences, shams, and superstitions. One reads *Crainquebille* and knows that in-
justice was anathema to his spirit. *L'Affaire Drey-
fus* brought Anatole France out of the groves of
his philosophic fancy, and *L'Anneau d'Amethyste*
was a contribution to Justice almost as potent as
Zola's *J'Accuse*. Though a declared Socialist, lat-
terly of an extreme type, he failed, as is usual with
men of letters, to influence politics. His direct indulgence in political propaganda stirred no waters. But
his diffused and temperamental criticism has cleared
away much superstition and deeply affected modern
thought.

Is one wrong in feeling that the goose "Modernity" is being cooked—modernity in the sense of the
spirit that makes of us *petits maîtres* trying for

startling expression of the trivial, for word-patterns unrelated to thought value, for the jazzy music of restive spirits? Is one misled in believing that we shall settle back into sober craftsmanship, with a disposition to look askance at these antics of our egos? Or is that wish mother to the thought? One would not deny to the fine bird Modernity some value, now that it is approaching the table. Given the war—it was an inevitable goose. From time to time these explosive periods occur. The spirit walks forth upon the waters, calling out to all to behold it, and, suddenly, with a cackle of surprise, disappears, leaving indeed a few ripples. In literature there is never really stagnation; the main current is all the time unobtrusively flowing on. The antics and splashings on the surface are sometimes excessive, sometimes scarcely visible. They are mostly made by little fish, for the big swim in their element with a certain concentration of purpose. You will have noticed how in painting movement succeeds movement, gets labelled, and becomes old-fashioned, leaving alive this master or that, around whom many had splashed and gambolled—a Turner, a Manet, a Millet, a Whistler, a Gauguin. So is it with Literature, and Time alone assesses the great surviving figures. Form is ever being subtly modified and changed, but it never really leaps. Reaction sees to that. No less than Life is Art organic, and the greater the artist the more he keeps to the main stream, and the natural rate of progression; the less he rushes and gushes or gets into backwaters and splashes away the summer's afternoon.

Art, even the art of the novel, has always been the subject of a "tug-of-war" between two schools of thought—the school that demands of it a revelation or criticism of life, and the school that asks of it nothing but pleasure-giving invention. Both schools, however, in the heat of their struggle for the possession of art tend to forget that, whether a work of art be critical and revealing, or a bit of decorative invention, its essence—that which makes it a work of art—is the presence of the mysterious quality called "life." And the conditions of "life" are: a sufficient relation of part to whole, and a sufficient flavouring of the artist's temperament. For only these elements give to a piece of work the essential novelty of a living thing.

A true work of art remains beautiful and living, though an ebb tide of fashion may leave it for the moment high and dry on the beach. It remains beautiful and living, simply because it has a life of its own. It may be a revelation of nature and human nature, like a drama of Euripides or a novel of Turgenev, or a bit of perfect fantasy like an Andersen fairy-tale, or a *Midsummer Night's Dream*—of such we do not think in terms of fashion.

The conflict, then, ever raging, whether or no a novelist's work should afford a criticism of life, is idle. Novelists run—as we say—in all shapes. De Maupassant, Turgenev, Conrad have been esteemed pure artists; Dickens, Tolstoi, France certainly have strong veins of the satirist or preacher in them. No one will deny the title "great novelist" to any one of the six; nor has the work of the three "pure artists" been devoid of critical value. Far from it. The fact is that all these six great novelists rendered life in terms of their own temperaments, and no novelist of their range and power of expression fails to be a critic of life. Even Flaubert, apostle of objectivity, æsthetic demi-god, passed profound criticism on life in his masterpieces *Un Cœur Simple, St. Julien l'Hospitalier,* and *Madame Bovary.* Whether, then, the picture be painted in seeming aloofness, or whether the novelist's self swoops on to and off the canvas, really doesn't matter much, for creative power and force of expression are the only real essentials.

The six great novelists whose profiles I have so lightly sketched are all humanists. The foodstuff for their powers has in each case been gathered from the wayward currents of human feeling, the varying pulses of the human heart, the countless ironic realities of human existence. Whatever formal creeds (if any) they may have endorsed, their real creed is summed up in the dwarf's saying: "Something human is dearer to me than the wealth of all the world."

There is nothing of the literary popinjay in any of them; and they were not theorists, no—not even Tolstoi—theorists who would fit humanity to a scheme or art to a pattern. Human life was relative to them before Professor Einstein discovered relativity. I think they all believed that means justify ends. And though that may be only half the truth

—like every proverb—it is the half suited to an age which has outworn dogma. Using the stuff of real life for the purposes of his art, a great novelist can, by the light he throws, forward the organic growth of human society, and colour the ethics of his time. He need not be conscious teacher or conscious rebel. He need only see widely, feel deeply, and be able to mould what he has seen or felt into that which has a new and significant life of its own. Did not the painter Manet say that the beginning of every new picture for him was like jumping into the sea without knowing how to swim? It is like that too for the novelist who pastures in the fields of human life. No patterns, no theories guide his efforts. He must discover. He must forge for himself out of life's raw material the design which suits.

Humanism is the creed of those who believe that, within the circle of the enwrapping mystery, men's fate is in their own hands, for better for worse; and these six novelists, by their natural absorption in all things human, and their great powers of expression, have furthered a faith which is becoming for modern man—perhaps—the only possible faith.

1923.

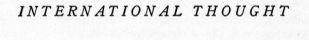

INTERNATIONAL THOUGHT

INTERNATIONAL THOUGHT

"The exchange of international thought is the only possible salvation of the world."

To those who, until 1914, believed in civil behaviour between man and man, the war and its ensuing peace brought disenchantment. Preoccupied with the humaner pursuits, and generally unfamiliar with the real struggle for existence, they were caught napping. The rest of mankind have experienced no particular astonishment—the doing-down of man by man was part of daily life, and when it was done collectively they felt no spiritual change. It was dreadful and—natural. This may not be a popular view of human life in the mass, but it is true. Average life is a long fight; this man's success is that man's failure; co-operation and justice are only the palliatives of a basic, and ruthless, competition. The disenchantment of the few would not have mattered so much but for the fact that they were the nerves and voice of the community. Their histories, poems, novels, plays, pictures, treatises, sermons, were the expression of what we call civilisation. And disenchanted philosophers, though by so much the nearer to the truths of existence, are by that much, perhaps, the less useful to human nature. We need scant reminder of a truth always with us, we need rather perpetual assertion that the truth might with advantage be, and may possibly with effort become, less unpleasant. Though we ought to look things in the face, afflatus is the essence of ethical philosophy.

It is a pity, then, that philosophy is, or has been, draggle-tailing—art avoiding life, taking to contraptions of form and colour signifying nothing; literature driven in on itself, or running riot; science more hopeful of perfecting poison gas than of abating coal-smoke or curing cancer; that religion should incline to tuck its head under the wing of spiritualism; that there should be, in fact, a kind of tacit abandonment of the belief in life. Sport, which still keeps a flag of idealism flying, is perhaps the most saving grace in the world at the moment, with its spirit of rules kept, and regard for the adversary, whether the fight is going for or against. When, if ever, the fair-play spirit of sport reigns over international affairs, the cat force which rules there now will slink away and human life emerge for the first time from jungle.

Looking the world in the face, we see what may be called a precious mess. Under a thin veneer—sometimes no veneer—of regard for civilisation, each country, great and small, is pursuing its own ends, struggling to rebuild its own house in the burnt village. The dread of confusion-worse-confounded, of death recrowned, and pestilence revivified alone keeps the nations to the compromise of peace. What chance has a better spirit?

"The exchange of international thought is the

only possible salvation of the world" are the words of Thomas Hardy, and so true that it may be well to cast an eye over such mediums as we have for the exchange of international thought. "The Permanent Court of International Justice"; "The League of Nations"; "The Pan-American Congress"; certain sectional associations of this nation with that nation, tarred somewhat with the brush of self-interest; sporadic international conferences concerned with sectional interests; and such societies as the Rotary International, the International Confederation of Students, and the P.E.N. Club, an international association of writers with friendly aims but no political intentions. These are about all, and they are taken none too seriously by the peoples of the earth. The salvation of a world in which we all live, however, would seem to have a certain importance. Why, then, is not more attention paid to the only existing means of salvation? The argument for neglect is much as follows: Force has always ruled human life—it always will. Competition is basic. Co-operation and justice succeed, indeed, in definite communities so far as to minimise the grosser forms of crime, but only because general opinion within the ring-fence of a definite community gives them an underlying force which the individual offender cannot withstand. There is no such ring-fence round nations, therefore no general opinion, and no underlying force to ensure the abstention of individual nations from crime—if, indeed, transgression of laws which are not fixed can be called crime.

This is the average hard-headed view at the moment. If it is to remain dominant, there is no salvation in store for the world. "Why not?" replies the hard-head. "It always has been the view, and the world has gone on!" True! But the last few years have brought a startling change in the conditions of existence—a change which has not yet been fully realised. *Destructive science has gone ahead out of all proportion.* It is developing so fast that each irresponsible assertion of national rights or interests brings the world appreciably nearer to ruin. Without any doubt whatever the powers of destruction are gaining fast on the powers of creation and construction. In old days a thirty years' war was needed to exhaust a nation; it will soon be (if it is not already) possible to exhaust a nation in a week by the destruction of its big towns from the air. The conquest of the air, so jubilantly hailed by the unthinking, may turn out the most sinister event that ever befell us, simply because it came before we were fit for it—fit to act reasonably under the temptation of its fearful possibilities. The use made of it in the last war showed that; and the sheeplike refusal of the startled nations to face the new situation, and unanimously ban chemical warfare and the use of flying for destructive purposes, shows it still more clearly. No one denies that the conquest of the air was a great, a wonderful achievement; no one denies that it could be a beneficent achievement if the nations would let it be. But mankind has not yet, apparently, reached a pitch of decency sufficient to be trusted with such an inviting and terribly destructive weapon. We are all familiar with the argument: Make war dreadful enough, and there will be no war. And we none of us believe in it. The last war disproved it utterly. Competition in armaments has already begun, among men who think, to mean competition in the air. Nothing else will count in a few years' time. We have made through our science a monster that will devour us yet unless by exchanging international thought we can create a general opinion against the new powers of destruction so strong and so unanimous that no nation will care to face the force which underlies it.

A well-known advocate of the League of Nations said the other day: "I do not believe it necessary that the League should have a definite force at its disposal. It could not maintain a force that would keep any first-rate power from breaking the peace. Its strength lies in the use of publicity; in its being able to voice universal disapproval with all the latent potentiality of universal action."

Certainly, the genuine publication of all military movements and developments throughout the world, the unfathoming and broadcasting of destructive inventions and devices, would bring us nearer to salvation than any covenant can do. If the world's chemists and the world's engineers would hold annual meetings in a friendly spirit for the salvation of mankind! If they could agree together that to exercise their ingenuity on the perfecting of destructive agents for the use of governments was a crime;

to take money for it a betrayal of their species! If
we could have such exchange of international
thought as that, then indeed we might hear the rustle
of salvation's wings. And—after all—why not? The
answer to the question—Is there to be happiness or
misery, growth or ruin for the human species?—
does not now lie with governments. Governments
are competitive trustees for competitive sections of
mankind. Put destruction in their hands and they
will use it to further the interests of those for whom
they are trustees; just as they will use and even
inspire the spiritual poison gas of pressmen. The
real key to the future is in the hands of those who
provide the means of destruction. Are scientists
(chemists, inventors, engineers) to be Americans,
Englishmen, Frenchmen, Germans, Japanese, Russians, before they are men, in this matter of the
making of destruction? Are they to be more concerned with the interests of their own countries or
with the interests of the human species? That has
become the question they have to answer now that
they have for the first time the future of the human
race within their grasp. Modern invention has taken
such a vast stride forward that the incidence of
responsibility is changed. It rests on Science as it
never did before; on Science, and on—Finance.
There again the exchange of international thought
has become terrifically important. The financiers of
the world, for instance, in the light of their knowledge, under the pressure of their difficulties, out of
the motive of mutual aid, could certainly devise

some real and lasting economic betterment, if only they would set to work steadily, not spasmodically, to exchange international thought.

Hard-head's answer to such suggestions is: "Nonsense! Inventors, chemists, engineers, financiers, all have to make their living and are just as disposed to believe in their own countries as other men. Their pockets and the countries who guarantee those pockets have first call on them." Well! That has become the point. If neither Science nor Finance will agree to think internationally, there is probably nothing for it but to kennel-up in disenchantment, and wait for an end which can't be very long in coming—not a complete end, of course, say a general condition of affairs similar to that which existed recently in the famine provinces of Russia.

It is easy to be pessimistic, and easy to indulge in cheap optimism; to steer between the two is hard. We still have a chance of saving and improving such civilisation as we have; but this chance depends on how far we succeed in exchanging international thought in the next few years. To some the word international has a socialistic, even communistic significance. But, as here used, it has nothing whatever to do with economic theories, class divisions, or political aims. The exchange of international thought, which alone can save us, is the exchange of thought between *craftsmen*—between the statesmen of the different countries; the lawyers of the different countries; the scientists, the financiers, the writers of the different countries. We have the mediums of exchange (however inadequately made use of) for the statesmen and the lawyers, but the scientists (inventors, chemists, engineers) and the financiers, the two sets of craftsmen in whose hands the future of the world chiefly lies, at present lack adequate machinery for the exchange of international thought, and adequate conception of the extent to which world responsibility now falls on them. If they could once realise the supreme nature of that responsibility, the battle of salvation should be half won.

Coming to the exchange of international thought in one's own craft, there seem three ways in which writers, as such, can help to ease the future of the world. They can be friendly and hospitable to the writers of other countries—and for this purpose exists the international P.E.N. Club, with its many and increasing branches. They can recognise and maintain the principle that works of the imagination, indeed all works of art, are the property of mankind at large, and not merely of the country of their origin; that to discontinue (for example) during a war with Germany the reading of German poetry, the listening to German music, the looking at German pictures, was a harmful absurdity which should never be repeated. Any real work of art, individual and racial though it be in root and fibre, is impersonal and universal in its appeal. Art is one of the great natural links (perhaps the only great natural link) between the various breeds of men, and to scotch its gentling influence in time of war is to confess ourselves still apes and tigers. Only writers can spread this creed, only writers can keep the door open for art during national feuds; and it is their plain duty to do this service to mankind.

The third and greatest way in which the writer can serve the future is simply stated in the words: Fair Play. The power of the Press is a good third to the powers of Science and Finance. If the Press, as a whole, never diverged from fair report; if it refused to give unmeasured service to party or patriotic passion; if it played the game as Sport plays it—what a clearance of the air! At present, with, of course, many and distinguished exceptions, the Press in every country plays the game according to rules of its own which have too little acquaintance with those of Sport.

The Press is manned by a great crew of writers, the vast majority of whom have in private life a higher standard of fair play than that followed by the Press ship they man. They would, I believe, be the first to confess that. Improvement in Press standards of international and political fair play can only come from the individual writers who make up the Press. And such reform will not come until editors and journalists acquire the habit of exchanging thought internationally, of broadening their minds and hearts with other points of view, of recognising that they must treat as they would themselves be treated. Only, in short, when they do as they would, most of them, individually choose to do, will a sort of word-miasma cease to breed international agues and fever. We do not commonly hold in private life that ends justify means. Why should they be held to justify means in Press life—why should report so often be accepted without due examination when it is favourable to one's views, rejected without due examination when it is unfavourable? Why should the other side's view be burked so often? And so on, and so on. The Press has great power and professes high ideals; it has much virtue; it does great service; but it does greater harm when, for whatever reason, it diverges from truth, or from the principles of fair play.

To sum up, Governments and Peoples are no longer in charge. Our fate is really in the hands of the three great Powers—Science, Finance, and the Press. Underneath the showy political surface of things, those three great Powers are secretly determining the march of the nations; and there is little hope for the future unless they can mellow and develop on international lines. In each of these departments of life there must be men who feel this as strongly as the writer of these words. The world's hope lies with them; in the possibility of their being able to institute a sort of craftsman's trusteeship for mankind—a new triple alliance, of Science, Finance, and the Press, in service to a new idealism. Nations, in block, will never join hands, never have much in common, never be able to see each other's points of view. The outstanding craftsmen of the nations have a far better chance of seeing eye to eye; they have the common ground of their craft, and a livelier vision. What divides them at present is a too narrow sense of patriotism, and—to speak crudely—money. Inventors must exist; financiers live; and papers pay. And, here, Irony smiles. Though Science, Finance, and the Press at present seem to doubt it, there is, still, more money to be made out of the salvation of mankind than out of its destruction; a better and more enduring livelihood for these three Estates. And yet without the free exchange of international thought we may be fairly certain that the present purely national basis of their livelihoods will persist, and if it does the human race will not, or at least so meagrely that it will be true to say of it, as of Anatole France's old woman: "It lives—but so little!"

1923.

ON EXPRESSION

AN ADDRESS

ON EXPRESSION*

EXPRESSION is my subject; and no mariner embarking on the endless waters of the Atlantic in a Canadian canoe could feel more lost than the speaker who ventures on a theme so wide and inexhaustible. And yet—how pleasant to know that it doesn't matter how one steers; for in no case can one arrive! The barque of discourse must needs be lifted every which way, veer helplessly in the winds and cross-currents of the measureless, and trace a crazy line.

Let me hazard, however, a prefatory axiom, about expression as a whole: The soul of good expression is an unexpectedness which, still, keeps to the mark of meaning, and does not betray truth. Fresh angles, new lights; but neither at the expense of significance, nor to the detriment of verity; never, in fact, just for the sake of being unexpected.

Following first the incorrigible bent of a novelist, let me proffer a speculation or two on the connection between expression and character-drawing. Hardly any figures in prose fiction seem to survive the rust of Time unless burnished by happy extravagance, saved by a tinge of irony, or inhabited by what one may call "familiar spirit." The creations of such

* Presidential Address to the English Association, 1924.

writers as Rabelais, Cervantes, Dumas, and Dickens
may serve to illustrate survival through happy extravagance; of Fielding, Jane Austen, Thackeray,
and Anatole France through ironical tincture; of
Tolstoi through "familiar spirit."

We all understand happy extravagance, however
incapable of it we may be; nor do we find any great
difficulty in appreciating the preservative qualities
of an ironic humour, which is very much a part of
English character. I need not, then, dwell on expression in regard to these. "Familiar spirit" is a
more mysterious affair. The characters in fiction
who are inhabited by "familiar spirit" are such as
convince the reader that he might meet and recognise them walking the everyday world. Mr. Hardy's
"Tess," Mr. Moore's "Esther," Mr. Bennett's
"Elsie" in *Riceyman Steps,* and Mr. Wells's "Kipps"
are good English specimens of characters so endowed. But one may gather more easily from
Tolstoi's creations in *War and Peace* and *Anna
Karenina,* than from any English examples, the nature of this quality. It demands an unself-conscious-
ness rare in English and French novelists—perfectly
simple expression, without trick, manner, or suspicion of desire to seem clever, modern, æsthetic.
Tolstoi was happily lost in the creative mood when
he made "Natasha," "Pierre," and "Anna."

"Familiar spirit," however, may inhabit a whole
book and ensure its permanence, although that book
contains no characters who remain in the mind:
Cranford, The Golden Age, The Purple Land occur

to me as instances. And probably the perfect example of "familiar spirit" permeating both book and its characters is Mark Twain's *Huckleberry Finn*—that joyous work as sure of immortality as any book I know. While on the question of resistance to Time, we ought, I suppose, to be wondering how much longer bulk is going to count in the equation of survival. Life driven by inventions from pillar to post has ever less time in its bank for us to draw on. But the persistent popularity of *Don Quixote, Tom Jones, David Copperfield, War and Peace,* and other very long masterpieces seems to contradict the logical suspicion that economy of expression must favour durability. The contemporary novel, at all events, shows little sign of shrinkage. Expression, taking the bit between its teeth, seems to be galloping on the road.

Ours, too, is an experimental epoch. New doctrines obtain. It has become, for instance, something of a fashion to feel that under the fevering influence of emotional stress we are all alike. Hero—they say—differs little from hero, when both are in pursuit of heroines. Villains have much in common, and are readily nosed in the lobby. Passion, in sum, is a leveller. Hence, the novelist's itch to express character without rise or fall in blood pressure—to bring out the individuality of the hero by subtle pictures of him changing his socks or putting in his clutch; of the heroine, by refining on her as she applies her lipstick, pours in her bath-salts, or leans out of the window into the summer night.

This undramatic mode has its drawbacks, and, so far perhaps, only two writers, neither of whom ever wrote a novel, have succeeded in using it to perfection—the Russian Tchehov and the English Katherine Mansfield. Their stories have a real past-mastership of everyday moments, of significant insignificances, and of differentiation through little in-between events. But by both of them this in-between method of expression was instinctively, I think, rather than self-consciously, adopted. It may be doubted whether they knew quite what they were aiming at—though certain words in Katherine Mansfield's diary show that she was approaching that knowledge when she passed from the world she loved and studied.

Among the experimentalists in expression, we cannot avoid noting, also, the psycho-analyst with his, or generally her, love of the worm in the bud, and prepossession with the past; an industrious and interesting method presided over by conscience in azure stockings and a handkerchief slightly scented with iodoform. These and other experimentalists have no doubt made an arrangement with Time to pass them through the Customs. But will they all escape confiscation? I quote a couple of paragraphs chosen at random from the work of a transatlantic writer, because a rising—nay, a risen—compatriot has termed her the most important pioneer in the field of letters in his time:

"When she was quite a young one she knew she had been in a family living and that that family living was one that any one could be one not have been having if they were to be one being one not thinking about being one having been having family living."

And this:

"All there is of more chances is in a book, all there is of any more chances is in a list, all there is of chances is in an address, all there is is what is the best place not to remain sitting, and suggesting that there is no title for relieving rising."

All modern writing, we are told by her compatriot, has sprung from experiments like these. Let me, however, read you a sentence written within twelve months by a writer, not ancient, who veils himself under the initials "Y.Y.":

"Hence I shall do my best to go on thinking well of hermit crabs. They are toys—grotesques that might be fitted into a fairy's thimble—as they traffic hither and thither with their borrowed houses on their backs, while the spotted jelly-fishes float above them in their long draperies and indolence."

Dare I profess to you my preference for this, and my doubt whether, modern though it be, it has any relation to those lauded experiments?

These samples, by the way, illustrate conveniently my opening axiom that the soul of good expression is an unexpectedness which still keeps to the mark of meaning, and does not betray truth. "In their long draperies and indolence"—of jelly-fish, how unexpected, and yet how true! But what of unexpectedness lies in those other quotations comes, it would seem, from a sedulous desire to be unexpected and futuristic at all costs.

This cult of the Future in art and letters. Futuristic! The very word is self-conscious. It suggests exhaustion of interest, and folk who won't be happy till they get the moon, and when they do are still more miserable. The true discoverer is of his own day absorbed in what he is doing. He stumbles upon novelty; and his nose is not turned up. But in the effort to free English from the tiresome habit of being contemporary, experiment in expression can step backwards instead of attempting to skip. In an age of newspapers, advertisements, captions, and political speeches, revolt against everyday expression is natural. With so much froth on the lips of contemporary style, young Hopeful suffers from reaction and walks, bowing backwards. I have in mind a recent instance—an ingenious and polished piece of work wrought in the English of an old master. A sort of pleasant false step that can be taken once with great effect, but cannot be repeated. For, however agreeable by way of a change may be the ring of older English, and however natural the surfeit in young critics of modern work, the fact remains that all great writers have made their names by expressing themselves in the diction, not of the past, but of their own day. Like the black footmen in the burlesque "Polly," we are all condemned to sing: "No retreat, no retreat; they must conquer or die who have no retreat." A little crossing with older English styles may do our modern English no harm, but the best writing of our time keeps itself supple and free from imitations, and endeavours, without mannerism, to express in words that ring new the writer's own temperament and vision. The great styles of the past cannot in the nature of things have a living unexpectedness for us of the present.

In sum, the less we try to form our English by self-conscious and definite experiments, keep our minds set towards the fresh, clear, supple expression of our visions, thoughts, and feelings, the greater the chance our English has of being fine. I make an exception, however, in favour of Income Tax forms and Acts of Parliament. A little self-conscious experiment on the part of their framers might at least enable us to understand them. Let me read you, at random, from a certain Lunacy Act:

"If, in the case of a lunatic being in a workhouse, the medical officer thereof does not sign such certificate as in sub-section 1 of this section mentioned or if at or before the expiration of fourteen days from the date of the certificate an order is not made under the hand of a Justice for the detention of the lunatic in the workhouse, or if after such an order has been made the lunatic ceases to be a proper person to be detained in a workhouse, the medical officer of the workhouse shall forthwith give notice in writing to a relieving officer of the Union to which the workhouse belongs that a pauper in the workhouse is a lunatic and a proper person to be sent to an asylum, and thereupon the like proceedings shall be taken by the relieving officer and all other persons for the purpose of removing the lunatic to an asylum, and within the same time, as by this Act provided in the case of a pauper deemed to be a lunatic and a proper person to be sent to an asylum, and pending such proceedings the lunatic may be detained in the workhouse."

Through long and painful study I can assure you that this really has a meaning; but is it any wonder that our asylums are full?

That breathless example of expression, by the way, dates from 1890, and I suggest that we can reasonably trace to it certain stopless modern experiments. Mark the rich crescendo of tumult towards the end, and the long periods for which one must sit with head in hands before glimmer of meaning will enter into it.

In short, expression, whether of laws, psychology, episode, or feeling, should be humane, and refrain from torturing the wits of mankind.

From Acts of Parliament it seems natural to turn to Shakespeare. Has Shakespeare inspired or discouraged the writer of English? His genius exhausted, as it were, the possibilities of expression. He even gave us our slang. When we say of a bore "Fire him out!" we do but follow Shakespeare. And that takes me off at a tangent. The incorporation of slang words—local, professional, even "family" slang words—into the language is, in reason, no bad thing. Slang is, at least, vigorous and apt. Probably most of our vital words were once slang; one by

one timidly made sacrosanct in despite of ecclesi-
astical and other wraths. For the beauty of a slang
word is that you need not put it in the dictionary,
it cries its own meaning to its own muffin-bell.

The mention of slang bends the mind almost insensibly towards the great American language; for
some, as you know, have claimed that the Americans already have a language of their own. Let us
avoid hyperbole. If Americans, with some exceptions, speak American, they still write English, and
generally very good English. Compare the dialogue,
for instance, in Sinclair Lewis's *Babbitt* with the
prose that lies in between; or listen to a play by
Eugene O'Neil, and then peruse the polished periods
of the late President Wilson. Certain Americanisms, too, are but Anglicisms which time has mur-
dered for us. Take for example the expression "His
first book *in* three years," where we should say
"His first book *for* three years." "I determined not
to play again *in* three months" may be met with in
the early Jacobean diary of Lady Anne Clifford.
Other "Americanisms" are English dialect words
almost lost over here; the very common American-
ism "dinky" will fall from the lips of a Dartmoor
farmer, than whom no one knows less of America.

We English have quite as much divergence between our spoken and our written language, with
this difference perhaps: Americans who talk in jar-
gon often write good English; but Britons who
speak the wondrous treble called cockney, and the
blurred ground-bass of the Yorkshire and Lanca-

shire towns, rarely express themselves at all in written words. And yet dare we condemn cockney—a lingo whose waters, in Southern England, seem fast flooding in over the dykes of the so-called Oxford accent, and such other rural dialects as are left?

And this brings me to a rather serious point: There is perhaps no greater divider of society than the difference in viva voce expression. If the East End on Hampstead Heath of a Bank Holiday pronounced its aitches, and said "Bai Jove! Isn't it ràther naice?"—or if, on the other hand, the West End dropped its aitches, and said "Aow! Look at the caows in the tryne!" should we not be very near to a social millennium? And this seems to invite the further question: Which of these two forms of English, cockney twang or the drawl of culchah, is the more desirable, as a national form of speech? The spirit of the age seems to favour cockney; and, certainly, it is glibber on the tongue. Place the offspring of culchad ducks under a cockney-speaking hen, and the ducklings will take to cockney as steel flies to a magnet. Cockney is infectious because it follows the line of least resistance, requiring far less effort of lips and tongue. Against cockney, then, with such adventitious advantages, the appeal must lie to the ear. To which of these two forms of speech is it pleasanter, or—shall we say—less maddening, to listen? If an unprejudiced Zulu were dropped into two circles of chatterers, the one in coster-town, the other in—well, not Oxford, for

Oxford is maligned—what would be the poor fellow's verdict? Who shall say?

At the present rate of cockney progress it will, however, not be long before your presidential address opens like this:

"A meriner navigytin' the endless waters of the gry Etlentic in a Canydian canoe could feel no more lorst than the speaker venturin' on a stunt laike this. An' yet aow pleasant to knaow that it daon't metter aow yer steer, for in no kyse can yer arrive."

If this is not desirable, our educational authorities will have to take in hand, even more seriously than at present, the subjugation of cockney in our national schools. And yet, would it be better if your milkman's boy said every morning: "Heah you are! A quart of milk, half a pound of buttah, and a bushel of eggs? That raight? Really! I'm fraightfully bucked. Good-bay!"

Perhaps some day our educational authorities may make both these forms of linguistic disease notifiable, and isolate the sufferers.

In the course of this digression I have mentioned the ear; and you will perhaps forgive me if I sideslip abruptly to the relative importance of ear and mind in lyric expression.

Take Shakespeare's "Out, out, brief candle!" Why is it charmed? Because of the vowel sounds? Or the dramatic unexpectedness of "brief" applied to "candle"? Or the image of the human spirit burning like a little flame, and blown into nothingness? Because of all three, I think, and in about equal proportions.

Or take Shelley's:

> "Mary dear, come to me soon,
> I am not well whilst thou art far;
> As sunset to the spherèd moon,
> As twilight to the western star,
> Thou, belovèd, art to me."

Again the vowel sounds: the unexpectedness of the word "far"; the imagery: to these must be added the emotion of longing. Wise, by the way, is a lyric poet when his appeal is short. Even Shelley would have been accounted far greater if he had left behind him only a picked tenth of his work. Lyric expression, in fact, can never afford to outrun its own strangeness. The following sonnet of Masefield's seems to me a fine expression of strange beauty:

> "Go spend your penny, Beauty, when you will,
> In the grave's darkness let the stamp be lost.
> The water still will bubble from the hill,
> And April quick the meadows with her ghost;
> Over the grass the daffodils will shiver,
> The primroses with their pale beauty abound,
> The blackbird be a lover, and make quiver
> With his glad singing the great soul of the ground;
> So that if the body rot, it will not matter;
> Up in the earth the great game will go on,
> The coming of Spring and the running of the water,
> And the young things glad of the womb's darkness gone.
>   And the joy we felt will be a part of the glory
>   In the lover's kiss that makes the old couple's story."

Note however that the last two lines exemplify—to me at least—that sudden emotional failure which blurs so much lyrical expression, even of the best poets.

The name Masefield brings up that form of expression known as the narrative poem. How far can verse do justice to a tale? The *Iliad,* the *Odyssey,* the *Canterbury Tales* were free from the rivalry of prose, for the prose narrative did not then apparently exist. The narrative poem to-day is a hybrid— like opera, that offspring of an unhappy marriage, for drama demands swiftness, music requires luxurious leisure; and a rich, long-drawn insistence at the top of the voice on emotions essentially sudden is characteristic of their child opera. Still, some mongrels are enchanting; who can resist the seduction of *Orfeo,* of *Carmen,* of *Pagliacci?* Opera "comes off" now and again, so does the narrative poem. It is, no doubt, a question of proportion. Just as water is H_2O, not H_3O—unless, indeed, it has changed in these impatient times—so a narrative poem must be just rightly balanced between the lyrical and the merely narrational. If there be too little percentage of lyrical beauty, we ask ourselves why, for the telling of a tale, verse, with its metrical handicap, was chosen, when free prose was to hand. Yet none of us would have *The Ancient Mariner*— that almost perfect narrative poem—expressed in prose: it is unthinkable.

> "The moving Moon went up the sky,
> And nowhere did abide;
> Softly she was going up,
> And a star or two beside——"

Unneighbourly people—poets! Using metres so perfectly that no one can use them again! An injunction should surely have been obtained to restrain George Meredith from writing *Love in the Valley.*

"When her mother tends her before the laughing mirror,
 Tying up her laces, looping up her curls——"

he jumped the claim of that metre in perpetuity. We owe grudges, too, against Fitzgerald for *Omar Khayyám* and Housman for *The Shropshire Lad;* and we never know when the next appropriation will be made. This is why poets have nervy temperaments, and more careful men go into the Law.

And while on the subject of lyrical expression it would seem fitting to consider what is known as journalese. Many journalists, of course, never stain their pages with that peculiar lyricism. And yet no event, I suppose, of dramatic moment occurs without the Press somewhere inflating the word-currency. The symptoms of journalese are the free use of clichés, and of artificial stimulation, through over-expression, gross or slight. It loves to say "largely," and that dreadful preposition "as regards," it dotes on any word with "cata" in it—catastrophe, cataclysm; battens on national fevers, and plays no small part in keeping a country's temperature above normal. It is highly infectious, and has been known to attack statesmen and other dignitaries. When journalese was at its rifest the Ministry of Health was established—possibly a coincidence.

But all over-expression, whether by journalists, poets, novelists, or clergymen, is bad for the language, bad for the mind; and by over-expression I mean the use of words running beyond the sincere feeling of writer or speaker or beyond what the event will sanely carry. From time to time a crusade is preached against it from the text: "The cat was on the mat." Some Victorian scribe, we must suppose, once wrote: "Stretching herself with feline grace, and emitting those sounds immemorially connected with satisfaction, Grimalkin lay on a rug whose richly variegated pattern spoke eloquently of the Orient and all the wonders of the Arabian Nights." And an exasperated reader annotated the margin with that shorter version of the absorbing event. How the late Georgian scribe will express the occurrence we do not yet know. Thus, perhaps: "What there is of cat is cat is what of cat there lying cat is what on what of mat lying cat." The reader will probably annotate the margin with "Some cat!"

But beside the verbose and florid runs another form of journalistic over-expression—the snappy head-line, which has attained as yet greater perfection in the glad atmosphere of America:

"Girl of thirteen, denied fine garb, tries death leap."
"Navy Board Holds Oil Quiz."
"Joke's on me says Angel of Film Star."
"Old man Stork a busy bird in Ruhr district."
"Acquitted murderer is through with girls."
"John T. King Highball hits Town."

Behind such galopading England still trails with leaden foot, hoping each year to overtake. "Hotspurs beat Blackburns" may yet become "Hots belt Blacks"; "Crippen hanged," "Ole man Crippen treads ether"; "Lord Palmerston unwell," "Pam punctured."

And is this perhaps the fitting moment to say a word about expression at Westminster? Eloquence, impromptu or prepared, is a gift which fills one, who lacks it, with a sort of reverence. And yet there is no denying that rhetoric is glib of tongue and knows not suspense. While rigmarole—like a man in a fog—goes round and round in a circle. Experience, listening, and reading suggests that the hypodermic syringe alone could put a period to rigmarole in a certain House. All a man has to say on a given subject can be said—they tell us—in twenty minutes. That is why I am taking an hour!—The dictum, in other words, is an exaggeration. Still, the biographies of statesmen abound in praises of superb orations; but when you read them you are often bored to tears by their prolixity, and wonder where those biographers could have been "raised." Chatham, Burke, Fox, Grattan, Bright, Gladstone, Disraeli—there is not one who did not constantly over-express himself and weaken the pith of his persuasion. Making every allowance for the customs of a House where Bills can still, it seems, be talked out, and members are obliged to speak lest other members should speak in place of them, there is still a rich margin of need for that considered brevity which, if not the soul of wit, is at least an aid to good and vigorous English, and a guarantee against sleep.

Having said so much about over-expression, you will expect me perhaps to touch on its antithesis. We English, for all our habit of dropping into poetry, are supposed to be an inexpressive race. There is some evidence. Consider, for instance, the Englishman speaking after dinner. He hums and haas, his eyes stare vacantly, he twiddles his buttons; and then, just as you are getting nervous that he is going to break down, you become conscious of a steady stream of sound; you are relieved, you lean back; you say "Hear, hear!" and the stream flows on, neither rising nor falling, just flowing, flowing; and slowly, slowly, you become nervous again—you look at your watch—oughtn't-er-oughtn't it to stop? But it-er-doesn't. Every five minutes you rouse yourself and murmur "Ha-ha!" And the stream flows on. You give it up, you sleep, and suddenly you hear: "But, ladies and gentlemen, I must not take up any more of your time." You rap the table, you seize your glass. But—lo!—he is off again! You apostrophise the Deity—in French; you yawn. He sees you, but it only seems to quicken the stream. And then, all at once, it stops. It has dried up, he is sitting down. And what has he said? What *has* he said? It has been a perfect example of under-expression.

But give an Englishman something to *do* in which he believes—for who can believe in speaking after dinner?—and he will do it with a minimum of talk; he will give you, in fact, another perfect example of verbal failure. Some few years ago painters coined the word "expressionism." When asked what they meant by it, they became involved and hot. Only fools—they thought—could mistake their meaning. Amazing number of fools in those days! At last a great good painter made it clear. Expressionism meant expressing the inside of a phenomenon without depicting its outside in a way that could be recognised. That is to say, if you wanted to express an apple-tree you drew and coloured one vertical and three fairly horizontal lines, attached a small coloured circle to one of these, and wrote the word "Fruity" in the catalogue. To express an Englishman by the expressionistic method you drew what resembled a pump, coloured it in a subdued manner, and wrote the words "Not working properly" in the catalogue.

I have not said anything, so far, about dramatic expression. The subject is delicate. When seeing a play, I am curiously absorbed in the dialogue—the interest, emotions, and suspense aroused by it. However birds may sing, streams flow, and thunders roll, on the stage; however luridly, austerely, symbolically classically, or realistically the scene be architectured, I am seeking the human figure and the words of his mouth—the "Out, out, brief candle!" And this is unfortunate, because dramatic expression through mere words seems to be going out of fashion. Cinema, revue, ballet, puppet show, and the architectural designer—all are in conspiracy to lower its importance. When enjoying a film, a ballet, a book by Mr. Gordon Craig I become uneasy. What if words are doomed—merely to be used to fill in the interstices of architecture, the intervals between jazz music, or just written on a board! What if the dramatist is to become second fiddler, a hack hired and commissioned! Shakespeare remarked: "The play's the thing!" We echo the saying, feel virtuous, and take our tickets for "The Three-Cornered Hat," "Lilac Time," "Charlie Chaplin," and "The Follies"; or, bemoaning the absence of British drama, sit down to wait for a National Theatre.

Do not, I beg, misunderstand me! Dialogue can be intolerable. Out of whole plays by noted dramatists half the words could be blotted with advantage. Many fourth acts would be better returned to the limbo of their authors' brains. And many characters have perished of their creators' theoretical loquacity! I stand by the definition I once gave, so rashly, for it has been accusing me of failure ever since: "Good dialogue is character . . . The art of writing true dramatic dialogue is an austere art, denying itself all licence, grudging every sentence devoted to the mere machinery of the play, suppressing all jokes and epigrams severed from character, relying for fun and pathos on the fun and tears of life. From start to finish, good dialogue is hand-made, like good lace; clear, of fine texture, furthering with each thread the harmony and strength of a design to which all must be subordinated."

189

It is curiously symptomatic of our variegated epoch that alongside the movement against dialogue plays are now and then written more full of polished and subtle conversation than ever plays have been. Such plays, however, though very interesting to read, hardly come under the heading of dramatic expression; they belong rather to a new form of psychological literature, intended, if not intentionally, for the study.

After all, there is no end to the extension of form —to the moulds into which we may run this language of ours, the greatest medium of expression in the world to-day. Including its American variety, the English language is the word-coin of well-nigh one hundred and seventy million white people, spread over nearly half the land surface of the earth. It is the language of practically every sea; the official tongue of some three hundred and fifty million brown and black and yellow people; the accredited business medium of the world; and more and more taught in South America, Japan, and some European countries.

For us private English folk who directly or indirectly are concerned with the welfare of the English language, there seems to be the duty of never losing sight of its world destiny. Surely we are not entitled to the slippered, unbraced word-garb of stay-at-homes; we need the attire of language braced and brushed, and fit to meet all glances. For our language is on view as never language was.

I often wonder, if only I didn't know English,

what I should think of the sound of it, well talked. I believe I should esteem it a soft speech very pleasant to the ear, varied but unemphatic, singularly free from guttural or metallic sounds, restful, dignified, and friendly. I believe—how prejudiced one is!—that I would choose it, well spoken, before any language in the world, not indeed as the most beautiful, but as the medium of expression of which one would tire last. Blend though it be, hybrid between two main stocks, and tinctured by many a visiting word, it has acquired rich harmony of its own, a vigorous individuality. It is worthy of any destiny, however wide.

The mind, taking a bird's-eye view of the English language from Chaucer to this day, noting the gradual but amazing changes it has undergone, will find it impossible, I think, to give the palm to any particular period in all those centuries. As with the lover of flowers who, through the moving seasons of the year, walks in his garden, watching the tulip and the apple blossom, the lilac, the iris, and the rose bloom in their good time, and cannot tell which most delights his eyes, nor when his garden reaches its full sweetness, so it is with us who love good English. Chaucer, Shakespeare, the makers of the Authorised Version, Defoe, Swift, Addison, Johnson, Burke, or Bright, you cannot crown the English of any one of these and say "Here the pinnacle was definitely reached." They were masters of expression, they used supremely well the English language of their days, tuning the instrument for their contemporaries, enlarging it for those who came after them. But the possibilities of this great organ of expression transcend even Shakespeare or the Bible. Dare we say that English is past its prime? Shall we accept defeat, and write the word decadent across the page? We cannot judge as yet the English of our day: we see the trees delicate or rank, leafy or dead in its bewildering wood, but the wood itself we cannot see. Every generation, and especially every English generation, is tempted to depreciate itself. This habit, however amiable and wholesome, is insincere, for there is in nearly all of us that which secretly stands by the age we live in.

I, at least, like to regard the English language as still in the making, capable of new twists and bold captures; and yet I think our attitude towards it should have more reverence; that we should love our mother tongue as we love our country, and try to express ourselves with vigour, dignity, and grace.

And so I end this wandering discourse with an affirmation of belief in the vitality, variety, the supple strength and subtle tones of our rich and ancient language; and of a hope that we may come to use it, man for man, woman for woman, speaking and writing, throughout our island, better than it has ever yet been used, with a fuller sense of its music and expressive power.

1924.

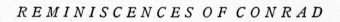

REMINISCENCES OF CONRAD

REMINISCENCES OF CONRAD

MANY writers knew my dead friend, and will write of him better than I; but no other writer knew him quite so long, or knew him both as sailor and novelist.

It was in March 1893 that I first met Conrad on board the English sailing ship *Torrens* in Adelaide Harbour. He was superintending the stowage of cargo. Very dark he looked in the burning sunlight—tanned, with a peaked brown beard, almost black hair, and dark brown eyes, over which the lids were deeply folded. He was thin, not tall, his arms very long, his shoulders broad, his head set rather forward. He spoke to me with a strong foreign accent. He seemed to me strange on an English ship. For fifty-six days I sailed in his company.

The chief mate bears the main burden of a sailing ship. All the first night he was fighting a fire in the hold. None of us seventeen passengers knew of it till long after. It was he who had most truck with the tail of that hurricane off the Leeuwin, and later with another storm. He was a good seaman, watchful of the weather, quick in handling the ship; considerate with the apprentices—we had a long, unhappy Belgian youth among them, who took unhandily to the sea and dreaded going aloft; Conrad compassionately spared him all he could. With the crew he was popular; they were individuals to him, not a mere gang; and long after he would talk of this or that among them, especially of old Andy the sailmaker: "I likéd that old fellow, you know." He was friendly with the young second mate, a cheerful, capable young seaman, very English; and respectful, if faintly ironic, with his whiskered, stout old English captain. I, supposed to be studying navigation for the Admiralty Bar, would every day work out the position of the ship with the captain. On one side of the saloon table we would sit and check our observations with those of Conrad, who from the other side of the table would look at us a little quizzically. For Conrad had commanded ships, and his subordinate position on the *Torrens* was only due to the fact that he was then still convalescent from the Congo experience which had nearly killed him. Many evening watches in fine weather we spent on the poop. Ever the great teller of a tale, he had already nearly twenty years of tales to tell. Tales of ships and storms, of Polish revolution, of his youthful Carlist gun-running adventure, of the Malay seas, and the Congo; and of men and men: all to a listener who had the insatiability of a twenty-five-year-old.

When, seven or eight years later, Conrad, though then in his best period and long acclaimed a great writer by the few, was struggling, year in year out, to keep a roof over him amidst the apathy of the many who afterwards fell over each other to read him in his worst period, I remember urging him to raise the wind by tale-telling in public. He wouldn't, and he was right. Still, so incomparable a *raconteur* must have made a success, even though his audience might have missed many words owing to his strange yet fascinating accent.

On that ship he talked of life, not literature; and it is *not* true that I introduced him to the life of letters. At Cape Town, on my last evening, he asked me to his cabin, and I remember feeling that he outweighed for me all the other experiences of that voyage. Fascination was Conrad's great characteristic—the fascination of vivid expressiveness and zest, of his deeply affectionate heart, and his far-ranging subtle mind. He was extraordinarily perceptive and receptive. Remembering his portraits of the simple Englishmen of action—the inexpressive Creightons, McWhirrs, Lingards, Bakers, Allistouns, and the half-savage figures of some of his books—we get some conception of the width of his sympathies when we read the following passages in a letter to me of February 1899 on the work of Henry James:

"Technical perfection, unless there is some real glow to illumine and warm it from within, must necessarily be cold. I argue that in Henry James there is such a glow, and not a dim one either; but to us, used, absolutely accustomed, to unartistic expression of fine headlong honest (or dishonest) sentiments, the art of Henry James does appear heartless. The outlines are so clear, the figures so finished, chiselled, carved and brought out, that we

exclaim—we, used to the shades of the contemporary fiction, to the more or less malformed shades—
we exclaim: 'Stone!' Not at all. I say flesh and
blood—very perfectly presented—perhaps with too
much perfection of *method*. . . . His heart shows
itself in the delicacy of his handling. . . . He is
never in deep gloom or in violent sunshine. But he
feels deeply and vividly every delicate shade. We
cannot ask for more. Not everyone is a Turgenev.
Moreover, Turgenev is not civilised (therein much
of his charm for us) in the sense Henry James is
civilised. *Satis.*"

From these sensitive words it is clear that he ap-
preciated the super-subtle, the ultra-civilised as completely as he grasped the life and thoughts of simple
folk. And yet there is not, so far as I can remember,
a single portrait in his gallery of a really subtle
English type, for Marlowe, though English in name,
is not so in nature.

Between his voyages in those last days of his
sailor's life Conrad used to stay at rooms in Gilling-
ham Street, near Victoria Station. It was there that
he read so prodigiously, and there that he suffered
from bouts of that lingering Congo fever which
dogged his health and fastened a deep, fitful gloom
over his spirit. In a letter to me he once said: "I
don't say anything of actual bodily pain, for, God
is my witness, I care for that less than nothing."
He was, indeed, truly stoical, and his naturally
buoyant spirit reacted with extreme suddenness. But
all the years I knew him—thirty-one—he had to

fight for decent health. Such words as "I have been
abominably ill—abominably is the right word,"
occur again and again in his letters, and his creative
achievement in a language not native to him, in face
of these constant bouts of illness, approaches the
marvellous.

It was the sea that, in my view, gave Conrad to the
English language. A fortunate accident—for he
knew French better than English at that time. He
started his manhood, as it were, at Marseilles. In a
letter to me (1905) he says: "In Marseilles I did
begin life thirty-one years ago. It's the place where
the puppy opened his eyes." He was ever more at
home with French literature than with English,
spoke that language with less accent, liked Frenchmen, and better understood their clearer thoughts.
And yet, perhaps, not quite an accident; for after all
he had the roving quality which has made the
English the great sea nation of the world; and, I
suppose, instinct led him to seek in English ships
the fullest field of expression for his nature. England, too, was to him the romantic country; it had
been enshrined for him, as a boy in Poland, by
Charles Dickens, Captain Marryat, Captain Cook,
and Franklin, the Arctic explorer. He always spoke
of Dickens with the affection we have for the writers
who captivate our youth.

No one, I take it, ever read the earliest Conrad
without the bewildered fascination of one opening
eyes on a new world; without, in fact, the feeling he
himself describes in that passage of *Youth,* where

he wakes up in an open boat in his first Eastern port, and sees "the East looking at him." I doubt if he will ever be surpassed as a creator of what we Westerners term "exotic atmosphere." The Malay coasts and rivers of *Almayer's Folly, An Outcast of the Islands* and the first pages of *The Rescue;* the Congo of *Heart of Darkness;* the Central Southern America of *Nostromo,* with many other land and seascapes, are bits of atmospheric painting *in excelsis.* Only one expression adequately described the sensations of us who read *Almayer's Folly* in 1894. We rubbed our eyes. Conrad was critically accepted from the very start; he never published a book that did not rouse a chorus of praise; but it was twenty years before he was welcomed by the public with sufficient warmth to give him a decent income.

Chance, in 1914—an indifferent Conrad—at last brought him fortune. From that year on to the end his books sold well; yet, with the exception of *The Secret Sharer* and some parts of *Victory,* none of his work in that late period was up to his own exalted mark. Was it natural that popular success should have coincided with the lesser excellence? Or was it simply an example of how long the strange takes to pierce the pickled hide of the reader of fiction? Or, still more simply, the undeniable fact that the reading public is more easily reached than it used to be?

It does disservice to Conrad's memory to be indiscriminate in praise of his work. Already, in reaction from this wholesale laudation, one notices a tendency in the younger generation to tilt the nose skyward and talk of his "parade." The shining work of his great period was before their time; it places him among the finest writers of all ages. Conrad's work, from *An Outcast of the Islands* to *The Secret Agent,* his work in *The Secret Sharer,* in the first chapters of *The Rescue* (written in 1898), and of some portions of *Victory,* are to his work in *The Arrow of Gold* and the last part of *The Rescue* as the value of pearl to that of mother-of-pearl. He was very tired toward the end; he wore himself clean out. To judge him by tired work is absurd; to lump all his work together, as if he were always the same Conrad, imperils a just estimate of his greatness.

I first re-encountered Conrad some months after that voyage when we paid a visit together to "Carmen" at Covent Garden Opera. "Carmen" was a vice with us both. It was already his fourteenth time of seeing that really dramatic opera. The blare of Wagner left him as cold as it leaves me; but he shared with my own father a curious fancy for Meyerbeer. In June 1910 he wrote: "I suppose I am now the only human being in these islands who thinks Meyerbeer a great composer; and I am an alien at that, and not to be wholly trusted." But music, fond though he was of it, could play no great part in a life spent at sea and, after his marriage in 1895, in the country. He went up to Town but seldom. He wrote always with blood and tears and needed seclusion for it.

A spurt was characteristic of Conrad's endings; he finished most of his books in that way—his vivid nature instinctively staged itself with dramatic rushes. Moreover, all those long early years he worked under the whip-lash of sheer necessity.

A sailor and an artist, he had little sense of money. He was not of those who can budget exactly and keep within it; and anyway he had too little, however neatly budgeted. It is true that his dramatic instinct and his subtlety would take a sort of pleasure in plotting against the lack of money, but it was at best a lugubrious amusement for one who had to whip his brain along when he was tired, when he was ill, when he was almost desperate. Letter after letter, talk after talk, unfolded to me the travail of those years. He needed to be the Stoic he really was.

I used to stay with him a good deal from 1895—1905, first at Stanford in Essex and then at Stanford in Kent. He was indefatigably good to me while my own puppy's eyes were opening to literature, and I was still in the early stages of that struggle with his craft which a writer worth his salt never quite abandons.

His affectionate interest was always wholly generous. In his letters to me, two to three hundred, there is not a sentence which breaks, or even jars, the feeling that he cared that one should do good work. There is some valuable criticism, but never any impatience, and no stinting of appreciation or encouragement. He never went back on friendship. The word "loyalty" has been much used by those who write or speak of him. It has been well used. He was always loyal to what he had at heart—to his philosophy, to his work, and to his friends; he was loyal even to his dislikes (not few) and to his scorn. People talk of Conrad as an aristocrat; I think it rather a silly word to apply to him. His mother's family, the Bebrowskis, were Polish landowners; the Korzeniowskis, too, his father's family, came, I think, of landowning stock; but the word aristocrat is much too dry to fit Conrad; he had no touch with "ruling," no feeling for it, except, maybe, such as is necessary to sail a ship; he was first and last the rover and the artist, with such a first-hand knowledge of men and things that he was habitually impatient with labels and pigeon-holes, with cheap theorising and word debauchery. He stared life very much in the face, and distrusted those who didn't. Above all, he had the keen humour which spiflicates all class and catalogues, and all ideals and aspirations that are not grounded in the simplest springs of human nature. He laughed at the clichés of so-called civilisation. His sense of humour, indeed, was far greater than one might think from his work. He had an almost ferocious enjoyment of the absurd. Writing seemed to dry or sardonise his humour. But in conversation his sense of fun was much more vivid; it would leap up in the midst of gloom or worry, and take charge with a shout.

Conrad had six country homes after his marriage, besides two temporary abodes. He wrote jestingly to my wife: "Houses are naturally rebellious and inimical to man." And, perhaps, having lived so much on ships, he really had a feeling of that sort. He certainly grew tired of them after a time.

I best remember Pent Farm at Stanford in Kent —that little, very old, charming, if inconvenient farmhouse, with its great barn beyond the yard, under the lee of the almost overhanging Pent. It was a friendly dwelling where you had to mind your head in connection with beams; and from whose windows you watched ducks and cats and lambs in the meadows beyond. He liked those quiet fields and that sheltering hill. Though he was not what we should call a "lover of nature" in the sense of one who spends long hours lost in the life of birds and flowers, of animals and trees, he could be vividly impressed by the charm and the variety of such things. He was fond, too, of Hudson's books; and no lover of Hudson's work is insensible to nature.

In Conrad's study at the Pent we burned together many midnight candles, much tobacco. In that house were written some of the *Youth* volume, *Lord Jim,* most of the *Typhoon* volume, *Nostromo, The Mirror of the Sea, The Secret Agent,* and other of Conrad's best work. Save that *The Nigger of the Narcissus* and the story *Youth* were written just before, at Stanford in Essex, the "Pent" may be said to synchronise with Conrad's best period. Kent was undoubtedly the county of his adoption, and this was the first of his four Kentish homes.

Many might suppose that Conrad would naturally settle by the sea. He never did. He had seen too much of it; like the sailor who when he turns into his bunk takes care that no sea air shall come in, he lived always well inland. The sea was no favourite with one too familiar with its moods. He disliked being labelled a novelist of the sea. He wrote of the sea, as perhaps no one, not even Herman Melville, has written; but dominant in all his writing of the sea is the note of struggle and escape. His hero is not the sea, but man in conflict with that cruel and treacherous element. Ships he loved, but the sea— no. Not that he ever abused it, or talked of it with aversion; he accepted it as he accepted all the inscrutable remorselessness of Nature. It was man's job to confront Nature with a loyal and steady heart —that was Conrad's creed, his contribution to the dignity of life. Is there a better? First and last he was interested in men, fascinated by the terrific spectacle of their struggles in a cosmos about which he had no illusions. He was sardonic, but he had none of the cynicism characteristic of small, cold-hearted beings.

He customarily laboured in the morning, and often would sit long hours over a single page. In 1906, when he was staying in our London house, he wrote to my wife: "I don't know that I am writing much in the little wooden house" (out in the garden), "but I smoke there religiously for three and a half hours every morning, with a sheet of paper before me and an American fountain-pen in my hand. What more could be expected from a conscientious author, I can't imagine."

In later years, when his enemy, gout, often attacked his writing hand, he was obliged to resort a good deal to dictation of first drafts. I cannot but believe that his work suffered from that necessity. But there were other and increasing handicaps—the war, which he felt keenly, and those constant bouts of ill-health which dragged at his marvellous natural vitality. I think I never saw Conrad quite in repose. His hands, his feet, his knees, his lips—sensitive, expressive, and ironical—something was always in motion, the dynamo never quite at rest within him. His mind was extraordinarily active and his memory for impressions and people most retentive, so that he stored with wonderful accuracy all the observations of his dark-brown eyes, which were so piercing and yet could be so soft. He had the precious faculty of interest in detail. To that we owe his pictures of scenes and life long past—their compelling verisimilitude, the intensely vivid variety of their composition. The storehouse of his subconscious self was probably as interesting and comprehensive a museum as any in the world. It is from the material in our subconscious minds that we create. Conrad's eyes never ceased snapshotting, and the millions of photographs they took were laid away by him to draw on. Besides, he was not hampered in his natural watchfulness by the preoccupation of an egoistic personality. He was not an egoist; he had far too much curiosity and genuine interest in things and people to be that. I don't mean to say that he had not an interest in himself and a belief in his own powers.

His allusions to his work are generally disparaging;
but at heart he knew the value of his gifts; and he
liked appreciation, especially from those (not many)
in whose judgment he had faith. He received more
praise, probably, than any other writer of our time;
but he never suffered from that *parvenu* disease,
swelled head; and "I," "I," "I" played no part in
his talk.

People have speculated on the literary influences
that for him were formative. Flaubert and Henry
James have been cited as his spiritual fathers. It
won't do. Conrad was a most voracious reader, and
he was trilingual. A Slav temperament, a life of
duty and adventure, vast varied reading, and the
English language—those were the elements from
which his highly individual work emerged. Not I,
who have so often heard him speak of them, will
deny his admiration for Flaubert, de Maupassant,
Turgenev, and Henry James; but one has only to
read Conrad's first book, *Almayer's Folly,* to per-
ceive that he started out on a path of his own, with
a method quite peculiar to himself, involuted to a
dangerous degree, perhaps, and I can trace no definite influence on him by any writer. He was as
different from Henry James as East from West.
Both had a certain natural intricacy and a super-
psychological bent, but there the likeness stops. As
for Flaubert—whom he read with constancy—that
conscientious Frenchman and determined stylist
could do nothing for Conrad except give him pleasure. No one could help Conrad. He had to subdue

to the purposes of his imagination a language that was not native to him; to work in a medium that was not the natural clothing of his Polish temperament. There were no guides to the desert that he crossed. I think perhaps he most delighted in the writings of Turgenev; but there is not the slightest evidence that he was influenced by him. He loved Turgenev's personality, and disliked Tolstoi's. The name Dostoievsky was in the nature of a red rag to him. I am told that he once admitted that Dostoievsky was "deep as the sea." Perhaps that was why he could not bear him, or possibly it was that Dostoievsky was too imbued with Russian essence for Polish appetite. In any case, his riderless extremisms offended something deep in Conrad.

I have spoken of his affection for Dickens. Trollope he liked. Thackeray I think not over much, though he had a due regard for such creations as Major Pendennis. Meredith's characters to him were "seven feet high," and his style too inflated. He admired Hardy's poetry. He always spoke with appreciation of Howells, especially of the admirable *Rise of Silas Lapham*. His affectionate admiration for Stephen Crane we know from his introduction to Thomas Beer's biography of that gifted writer. Henry James in his middle period—the Henry James of *Daisy Miller, The Madonna of the Future, Greville Fane, The Real Thing, The Pension Beaurepas*—was precious to him. But of his feeling for that delicate master, for Anatole France, de Maupassant, Daudet, and Turgenev, he has written in his *Notes on Life and Letters*. I remember, too, that he had a great liking for those two very different writers, Balzac and Merimée.

Of philosophy he had read a good deal, but on the whole spoke little. Schopenhauer used to give him satisfaction twenty years and more ago, and he liked both the personality and the writings of William James.

I saw little of Conrad during the war. Of whom did one see much? He was caught in Poland at the opening of that business, and it was some months before he succeeded in getting home. Tall words, such as "War to end War" left him, a continental and a realist, appropriately cold. When it was over he wrote: "So I send these few lines to convey to you both all possible good wishes for unbroken felicity in your new home and many years of peace. At the same time I'll confess that neither felicity nor peace inspire me with much confidence. There is an air of 'the packed valise' about these two divine but unfashionable figures. I suppose the North Pole would be the only place for them, where there is neither thought nor heat, where the very water is stable, and the democratic bawlings of the virtuous leaders of mankind die out into a frozen, unsympathetic silence." Conrad had always a great regard for men of action, for workmen who stuck to their last and did their own jobs well; he had a corresponding distrust of amateur omniscience and handy wise-acres; he curled his lip at political and journalistic protestation; cheap-jackery and claptrap of all sorts drew from him a somewhat violently expressed detestation. I suppose what he most despised in life was ill-educated theory, and what he most hated, blatancy and pretence. He smelled it coming round the corner and at once his bristles would rise. He was an extremely quick judge of a man. I remember a dinner convoked by me, that he might meet a feminine compatriot of his own married to one who was not a compatriot. The instant dislike he took to the latter individual was so full of electricity that we did not dine in comfort. The dislike was entirely merited. This quick instinct for character and types inimical to him was balanced by equally sure predilections, so that his friendships were always, or nearly always, lasting—I can think of only one exception. He illustrated vividly the profound truth that friendship is very much an affair of nerves, grounded in instinct rather than in reason or in circumstance, the outcome of a sort of deep affinity which prevents jarring. His Preface to the *Life of Stephen Crane* supplies all the evidence we need of Conrad's instantaneous yet lasting sympathy with certain people; and of his instant antipathy to others. It contains also the assurance that after he became a writer he "never kept a diary and never owned a note-book"—a statement which surprised no one who knew the resources of his memory and the brooding nature of his creative spirit.

"Genius" has somewhere been defined as the power to make much out of little. In *Nostromo* Conrad made a continent out of just a sailor's

glimpse of a South American port, some twenty
years before. In *The Secret Agent* he created an
underworld out of probably as little actual experience. On the other hand, we have in *The Nigger*, in
Youth and *Heart of Darkness* the raw material of his
own life transmuted into the gold of fine art. People,
and there are such, who think that writers like
Conrad, if there be any, can shake things from
their sleeve, would be staggered if they could have
watched the pain and stress of his writing life. In
his last letter to me but one, February 1924, he says:
"However, I have begun to work a little—on my
runaway novel. I call it 'runaway' because I've been
after it for two years (The Rover is a mere inter-
lude) without being able to overtake it. The end
seems as far as ever! It's like a chase in a nightmare—weird and exhausting. Your news that you
have finished a novel brings me a bit of comfort.
So there are novels that *can* be finished—then why
not mine? Of course I see 'fiction' advertised in the
papers—heaps of it. But published announcements
seem to me mere phantasms . . . I don't believe
in their reality." There are dozens of such allusions
to almost despairing efforts in his letters. He must,
like all good workmen, have had his hours of com-
pensation; but if ever a man worked in the sweat
of spirit and body it was Conrad. That is what
makes his great achievement so inspiring. He hung
on to his job through every kind of weather, mostly
foul. He never shirked. In an age more and more
mechanical, more and more given to short cuts and

the line of least resistance, the example of his life's work shines out; its instinctive fidelity, his artist's desire to make the best thing he could. Fidelity! Yes, that is the word which best sums up his life and work.

The last time I saw Conrad—about a year ago—I wasn't very well, and he came and sat in my bedroom, full of affectionate solicitude. It seems, still, hardly believable that I shall not see him again. His wife tells me that a sort of homing instinct was on him in the last month of his life, that he seemed sometimes to wish to drop everything and go back to Poland. Birth calling to Death—no more than that, perhaps, for he loved England, the home of his wandering, of his work, of his last long landfall.

If to a man's deserts is measured out the quality of his rest, Conrad shall sleep well.

1924.

BOOKS AS AMBASSADORS

BOOKS AS AMBASSADORS

Have books done more to unite or to divide mankind? Have not the Bible, the Koran, and *Das Kapital,* notwithstanding their intentions, divided men more than all other books whatsoever have united them?

"I come not to bring peace but a sword," could be written with truth on the covers of a multitude of books, and the sentiment "Books as Ambassadors" must be qualified by as many saving clauses as an Act of Parliament.

We can acquit Euclid, and books on the condition of the moon, of making mischief; we can assert with safety that the works of Euripides, Virgil, Petrarch, Shakespeare, Goethe, Montaigne, Cervantes, Dante have been positively unifying.

We may indeed go further and lay it down that any book which is a work of art and rouses impersonal emotion bears out this motto. Unhappily, much literature which has the quality of art is dreadfully diminished in translation. Poetry, and fiction with individual style, with flower of author in it, lose much when rendered out of their native garb. And these are just the books which most help to join the hearts of men, for they constantly remind

us that within each Italian, each Pole, each Englishman, Russian, Frenchman, Austrian, Swede there
is a human being who varies as little in essentials
as bulldog from poodle-dog, whose life is the same
tragi-comedy, whose appetites, virtues and defects
are neither more nor less appalling, and who, when
his clock strikes, will pass through the same dark
doorway.

Shakespeare's *Lear* and Balzac's *Père Goriot,*
Tolstoi's *Anna* and Goethe's *Gretchen* bring the
souls of readers to the same sweet waters. The same
bright angels pass above us all when we hold our
breath at the death of Bazarov, at the lovering of
Romeo, at the divine madness of the immortal Don.
When books are made in the large and welcoming
spirit of Art they distil a balm into the parched
human soul, and dispose it to gentilesse.

Dickens with his novels, Andersen with his fairy
tales, a thousand and one other writers with their
fancy folk have put a daub of cement between the
bricks of human life, and traversed all national
boundaries with every word they wrote. Far be it
from this writer to decry or minimise the beneficent
power of Literature when it can, even by some
stretching of the imagination, be called Art. Than
Art there is no greater mollifying force. None, indeed, so great. And we may go even further still
and say that any book which, without exciting partisanship, hatred or contempt, familiarises us with
what lies outside our normal experience will add to
the pool of human unity by binding mind to mind

with the cement of knowledge. *Encyclopedia Britannica,* the *Latin Grammar, Reading Without Tears,* Vasari's *Lives of the Painters* and the *Child's Guide to Knowledge,* are impeccably on the credit side.

Thousands of harmonising books—yes. But do they pull the balance down?

Ink is cheap, and man disposed to prejudice, to restless curiosity, to wrath, and partisanship. He lets loose currents of ink beyond his ken or his control. Hourly comes a fellow with some sacred bee in his bonnet, writes its buzzing down, and sets men by the ears. *The Divine Comedy* counts little beside the treatise of a Treitschke, when nitro-glycerine has been paid for and is waiting to be used. Praise of the arch-disturber Napoleon may be bought at half-a-crown the ream. Jingoes, Chauvinists, Pan-Whatnots find willing publishers, a Press to pat their backs, and Publics with the ears, but not the sense, of Balaam's ass.

And books—so well intentioned—have a way of familiarising us with horrors till we feel quite cosy about them. We grow inured to the idea of perishing wholesale, town by town, from poison gas dropping like the gentle dew from heaven, with possibly more noise, but certainly less warning. Books tell us that this is the natural course of the human serial, and gradually we think: "Dear me! Very awkward, but I suppose it is. Why worry?" And when some bright logician, in a tome at 5s. net, asks: "What is the matter with poisoning water supplies or disseminating the germs of typhus? It's all of a piece with nitro-glycerine," we very soon think: "Well, what is the matter with it, anyway? War is war!" So it goes. Of course such books might be burned at birth, but then—they're not. *The Little Flowers of St. Francis* might be put into the hands of Labour, instead of *Das Kapital*—but is it?

No! Books will be books! Peace-making or belligerent, like men.

And the schism-working books are all written by such admirable fellows, confident that they are doing God's work and opening the eyes of mortals. How can one remonstrate with the patriotic soldier, whose simple stare has never seen anything but the good of his own country, when he recommends that country to commit any frightfulness, so long as it is detrimental to the enemy? It would be unkind. The man does his best. He has his lights. Or how reconcile it with freedom of speech and liberty of subject to incarcerate the poet who hales his country over hill, over dale, thoro' brake thoro' briar, to glorious conquest? It isn't done. On the contrary, indeed. And the industrious, the self-sacrificing scientist, who works and writes in the faith that knowledge justifies all—how dash from his lips the chalice of that credulity? Above all, the visionary, single-minded soul, who sees his vision and naught else, for whom the world is well lost in flood and fury, if his creed prevail—have we the heart so to dilute his ink that it becomes illegible? Not so. He, like the earthquake, has his uses.

We must suffer these—we must suffer from them and their books.

"Books as ambassadors"—well, yes! But ambassadors, before now, have been known to put the fat in the fire!

1924.

TIME, TIDES, AND TASTE

TIME, TIDES, AND TASTE

THE tides of taste flow and ebb and flow again, and works of "genius" and "art" pop in and out of fashion like little men on old-time clocks. So that a watcher, even in one brief generation, acquires a wholesome cynicism, eyes dog-wise the criticism of the day, the cults of the clever, the enthusiasms of the young. He learns that experiment and achievement are not quite interchangeable terms. The shortness of life and the length of art are to him increasingly apparent, and he has come to mistrust the inveterate cock-eyed cocksureness of the literary man.

Save as museum pieces in the unvisited rooms of the Past, how very few books live! In the whole range of English literature down to 1800, who, except by professors and their pupils as part of education, is widely read? Shakespeare. Save for some dozen or so still well-thumbed volumes, the others— even Chaucer, Bunyan, Milton, Dryden, Johnson, Defoe, Swift, Fielding, Locke, Jeremy Taylor—are but venerable names. Of all the great writers in English, poets and novelists of the nineteenth century, who are now really *coram populo?* Dickens, Stevenson, and Mark Twain; with Shelley, Scott, Wordsworth, Jane Austen, Trollope, and Tennyson, dipped into; and the readers of such as Byron,

Hawthorne, Thackeray, Poe, the Brontës, Marryat, Charles Reade, Browning, Blackmore, Artemus Ward, Whitman, Herman Melville, confined to two or three surviving books apiece. I speak not here of connoisseurs, students, or bookworms, but of the reading public at large. Even Meredith, Swinburne, Howells, and Henry James are passing already from the minds of those who read for pastime. Who among the living will fare better? Shall we not drift into dusty limbo, at best remembered as names, or each by a book or two—a *Tess,* an *Esther Waters,* a *Mr. Polly,* a *Babbitt,* an *Ethan Frome,* an *Old Wives' Tale,* a *Reynard the Fox.* And in the twilight of this reflection the number of "great" books that appear every year, the annual "geniuses," have but a sober hue. The wheel turns and they fly off like the powdery dust of high summer.

In this general certainty of extinction the future is hardly worth considering by writers. We are of our day. Lamb-like, we kick our heels in the spring; and, if lucky, are still served with mint sauce, instead of currant jelly, in the autumn. On the stage, lately, they performed a skit of the high-kicking dances that adorned English Gaiety burlesques in the late eighties—a row of young women, over-rouged, over-wigged, and under-frilled, trying with an intent and solemn diligence to reach high heaven with their toes. With what utter and expressionless precision their legs went up—and up—and up! We remembered the original and the pleasure it then gave us! Dear me! Our taste had changed.

Yes, the Eighties are paved over, and the grass grows between; but they were vital while they lasted —as vital as these Twenties, who must themselves become a grass-grown walk. Remember the Nineties and their Yellow Book—how it glittered and it shone—not Bloomsbury in all its glory puts on so many frills. And where are those Nineties now? To think that our high-spirited Twenties, with their absolute taste, will be the "gone-offs" of the Thirties, the "old geysers" of the Forties! Professor Einstein, who with such careful ceremony, married "relativity" to a world which had in secret always enjoyed it, left to youthful æsthetes his cast-off "absolute," so that—if not precisely in unity—they might dwell together, decade by decade, unrelated in their taste to time and tide.

The first years of this century turned the moon over, too; were as absolute as these Twenties, and as clever. They met, shook a leg, put out a tongue, and lo! their elders did not exist—at least for the moment. There was Hardy! Let us see what happened to the poor man. They labelled him old-fashioned, and out he went, but—he came in again. There was Stevenson, that mere Romantic—how many deaths he died on their lips! And how alive he still is! There was Kipling—oh, poor Kipling! There was Barrie—a sad case! There was Shaw— that shocking journalist! And then those smart young "absolutes" lost their innocence, passed into relativity, and now are the merest "geysers" themselves. There were sucking "geniuses" in those days, too, but they all died young, killed by the "geniuses" who followed. Layer on layer the ages lie, each as innocent as the one before, and each happy while it lasts, under its midnight lamps, putting the Past in its place, and that a little lower than its own, monopolising style, and with serene finality pronouncing: "This is 'done,'" or "That is drivel."

Those periodic makers of new forms—canonised and pedestalled by coterie—how little they shake the world of letters! They are like novelists who enter the British House of Commons to reform society, and leave it—oh! so soon—with nothing but themselves reformed. You remember a certain Mr. Carlyle who purposed to renovate style? Ah! what a to-do! But when he was through, there were only his works and your smile. Since then there have been others—this decade boasts at least three—and when it passes, so will they, clad lightly in a general grin. For if anything is certain in the mystery which surrounds literary survival, it is this: The "precious" has precious little chance. Was there anything exotic, self-conscious in their day, about the expression of any among those who have eluded Time so far? Of Homer, say—if ever Homer was —or the Greek dramatists; of Virgil, Horace, Plutarch, Dante, Montaigne, Shakespeare, Cervantes, Goethe, Tolstoi? These outran no constables. That is worth a thought before falling on our knees in front of the Messieurs Petitmaitre or Madame Soubresaut. Calm, unruffled, all-absorbing, the main stream of literature flows, and makes of each little tributary decade, which takes itself for eternity, about as much as a trout makes of a single mayfly.

But the cry of literary Youth: "Crown taste in our time, O Lord! We are 'the goods'!" is welcome. Without the two-year-olds, their breeding, paces, colour, trials, performance, the literary papers would be starved. Lacking discovery of new flyers and discovery that old flyers never could fly, contemporary criticism could not sing with Macheath:

> "I sip every flower,
> I change every hour!"

And how amusing to watch the wheel of criticism turning—to see a Dostoievsky displace a Turgenev, a Tchehov displace both; a Dreiser replace a Norris, a Lewis a Dreiser, Un Tel a Lewis, a Dreiser Un Tel; a Proust displace a France, and a Joyce replace the Deity!

Once on a time an English editor in a single discharge blew from his mouth every literary name alive, and died editorially in the blast. This was perhaps the most striking example of time-and-trouble-saving in all the history of literature. Why spend ten years in sapping what can be blasted in a day without any sapping at all, especially when the result is the same in both cases! For literary fame—not the brand in publishers' advertisements, nor the bayleaf grown in cafés, but that which clings on, though blasted every other decade—is mysteriously entwined with public favour, and curiously detached from critical pronouncement. Like ivy, it gets slow

227

hold, climbs up a writer, spreads in a mass of decorative leaf, and sometimes chokes the creative life out of him. Take the strange case of Conrad, who during the first eighteen years of his writing life was praised by critics as writers seldom have been, yet was hardly known to the public; and then, in a quick three years, was covered with the leaves of fame. Take the case of Kipling, critically acclaimed, critically condemned, again acclaimed, again condemned, and strangely famous all the time. Contemporary taste sways with action and reaction, obeys a dislike of repetition, a craving for novelty; follows the talk of the most self-conscious literary clique of its day, and swims with the tide of worldly circumstance, such as a pre-war or an after-war mood; it is policed only by a sense of proportion in the general mind, which all the time manages to rescue from the ebb and flow of taste what really feeds and amuses it. The mental appetite of literary youth changes almost every year; the mental appetite of simpler folk remains much the same for a generation at least; and certain primal food-demands of the mind last down the centuries: Item, the craving for drama, which is satisfied by the telling of a tale; item, the craving for seeing yourself and your neighbour reproduced, which is satisfied by the creation of character. The period whose taste gets away from these simple demands is found in the long run no tributary, however it may have raced and bubbled to all seeming, but just a backwater.

The present period, very sparkling, unquestionably self-conscious and inclined to proclaim its monopoly of cleverness, will contribute, but not by virtue of its opinion of itself, nor by reason of its extravagant experiments. The Forties will not write —nay, nor even the Thirties—in the style of Mr. Dotter and Mrs. Dasher of the Twenties; the Thirties will put in stops again, with other old-fashioned aids to the brain, such as coherence and a certain connection between words and thought. Violent changes, which are "the thing" from time to time, should at least be based on practical advantage. Take the change in dancing, for example; it has two very practical—dare we say?—advantages; it causes less perspiration, and establishes closer contact between male and female. But the stopless and the "bide-a-wee-thorn" writers of to-day cause more perspiration and establish a wider space between themselves and their readers. They require more time and patience, but readers have ever less of both. Stopless and Bide-a-wee-thorn will end by taking in each other's washing, and with no circle of adorers to see how they do it. This, indeed, is a sure thing. But Stopless and Bide-a-wee-thorn, however earnest their own convictions that they are pioneers to a more precious future, are mere stunt customers. By them To-day will not be judged. No! To-day will count because, like most periods, it has some genuine creative talent, some real power of telling a tale, and some quiet devotion to its job. It will count in spite of that proclaimed cleverness which is perhaps only speed. The ball flies more lightly—the "wickets are faster," as we say; hit or get out is the watchword. But the result? Will Time give the palm to the team of to-day over the team of ten, twenty, thirty years ago? Maybe—for there never were so many players of the writing game as now. They jostle up like young larch trees planted too close together; and some will shoot ahead and be spared for a time, as ornamental timber, when the Great Forester converts the covert into pit-props.

But as to the claim, seemingly implicit in café-table talk, that some fresh human faculty has been aroused, that there is a real new demand of the mind, which the old writers, painters, and composers cannot satisfy—let us consider! Applause now greets a piece of decorative noise such as Honegger's rendering of a locomotive's progress. But even in the time of Bach would not Honegger or Stravinsky—provided they escaped incarceration—have stimulated the eighteenth-century man by their ingenious noises fully as much as the beating of forest drums has always stimulated people? Down to quite a short time ago a white man who craved for exciting noise had to repair to the Zoos at feeding-time, or hire a man to play the bagpipes without actually breaking into a tune. Such considerable and not undignified sounds were all he could obtain, but his appetite was there; all unknowingly he hungered for *Le Sacre du Printemps.* So in literature—the reader down to 1910 was forced to glut his cravings for the symptomatic and the well-nigh unintelligible, on medical treatises, and the differential calculus; now he can take down a novel. Many who went about looking at pictures and sculpture in the last century loved also to see cranes at work, engines giving off steam, scaffolding at night-time, piles of beetroot, and the simple village pump; there was a craving within them that pictures and sculpture did not satisfy—whereas now it is different.

No, this new faculty and demand is probably *not* at all new. To-day is simply satisfying an old craving in a different and more compendious fashion. People have been known to affirm that the new music, art, literature are mere noise, pattern, and mental exercise; but that is very rude and old-fashioned! The new art, music, and literature—I speak of their exotic blossoms—satisfy certain emotional or mental desires which hitherto could get no food from art. To be able to call art that which we used not to call art must surely give us a broader satisfaction, or at least put a higher premium on our lower cravings. It widens, if it does not heighten, our conception of æstheticism, to include among the æsthetic, the child, the savage, the mathematician, the medical man—very considerable sections of the population—hitherto excluded. Probably we shall never again let these new æsthetes slip altogether from the company of the elect—though in the Thirties and Forties we may not place them quite so high in the scale of taste.

Yes, on the whole we must reject the theory of a new faculty in the modern mind, and fall back on a simple shift of categories. The human being doesn't change so quickly as all that, but labels are always getting swapped around; and, in that activity, To-day is highly active and adventurous, if possibly a little intoxicated and calisthenic. But, to risk a repetition: To-day will be remembered for more substantial reasons than its cocktails and its calisthenics. And since, in any case, like other periods, it must pass, shall it not kick as high as it can, while yet living? The certainty of decease is an incentive to vitality in the well-constituted mind. To be alive and, as Mr. Verdant Green used to say, "prou' title," is the keystone of philosophy. Let Time do his worst! The Twenties do well to defy him. For no matter how many candles they burn, judgments pronounce, or policies of insurance take out, that Old Blighter Time will have his way with them in the end.

1925.

FAITH OF A NOVELIST

TRUTH, to human beings, is the same just relation of part to whole as that without
which a living thing will not function. And
the task before creative writers is the presentation
of visions with the implicit proportions of truth, and
so coloured by the temperament of their seers as to
have the essential novelty of living things—for no
two living things are alike, nor any two ways of
seeing them similar.

A work of fiction, then, should carry the hall-
mark of its author so surely as a Goya, a Daumier,
a Velasquez, and a Mathew Maris are, as a rule,
the unmistakable creations of those masters. This
is not to speak of the tricks and manners that attract
that facile elf the caricaturist, nor to imply that a
novel should be a sort of sandwich, in which the
author's mood or philosophy is the slice of ham.
It is, rather, a demand for a subtle impregnation of
flavour; an individual way of seeing and feeling
such as, for instance, makes de Maupassant a more
poignant and fascinating writer than his master
Flaubert, and Dickens more living and permanent
than George Eliot.

Some hold that the artist's sole function is the
impersonal elucidation of the truths of Nature. But
for the purposes of Art there are no such things as

truths of Nature, apart from the individual vision of the artist. Seer and thing seen, inextricably involved one with the other, form the texture of any masterpiece. And such subtle intermingling of seer with thing seen is the outcome only of long and intricate brooding, a process not too favoured by modern life, yet without which we achieve little but a fluent chaos of clever insignificant impressions, a kind of glorified journalism.

The temperament of any considerable novelist is not likely to be a simple equation. The emotional and critical sides of his nature will be ever fighting a duel, first one then the other getting the upper hand, and too seldom fusing into the balance of a drawn battle. And, according as the tides sway, so will be the effect on the reader. A novelist must ever wish to discover a member of the Public who, never yet having read a word of his writing, would submit to the ordeal of reading him straight through. Probably the effect could only be judged through an autopsy; but in the remote case of survival it would be profoundly interesting to the novelist to see the difference, if any, produced in his reader's outlook over life. Since, however, there is a limit to human complaisance, he may never know the exact measure of his infecting power; or whether, indeed, he is not just a long soporific.

But no novelist who believes in giving value to his temperament will be always soporific. That which gets on his nerves will surely out, and more especially when his theme deals with the honeycomb we call Society. To think that birth, property, position, worldly superiority—in sum—is anything but a piece of good luck may be out of date, but Society takes itself for granted very subtly, and there is still little of a genuine "There, but for the grace of God, go I!" feeling in those who do not have to slave, struggle, and cadge for their livings; little power of seeing themselves as they might so easily have been but for their good fortune, little of the ironic eye, turned in as well as out. Quite modest and unassuming specimens in the upper sections of the honeycomb accept quietly, blindly, blandly, themselves, their clothes, habits, accent, manners, morals. This very deep, unconscious Pharisaism is to be found fitting like a skin on aristocrats professing the most democratic sentiments, on pastors proclaiming the most Christian doctrines, on intellectuals redolent of culture—so natural is it, so almost physical, so closely connected with the nerves of nose, and eyes, and ears.

The inevitable tendency, then, of the novelist who deals with social types, if he sees things in due proportion, will be to skin the knuckles of privilege.

A saying that used to be met with in almost every review of a novel was this: "The part of the artist is to see life steadily and to see it whole." It was generally used when a writer did not see life as his critic saw it, or when he implied that there was anything rotten in the state of Denmark.

But to "see life steadily and to see it whole" is certainly not to see it with the eye of an established order, self-contented and contained. A section of life seen without relation to the rest of life has no perspective; is flat like a pancake. And such flatness in presentment is characteristic of the second-rate novelist. Another saying that used to be met with on the same page was this, "A work of art should be a criticism of life," which means nothing if not that an artist should see life with his individual or temperamental eye. It may be his misfortune, but is hardly his fault, if that eye does not take a complacent view of existence.

That those incompatibles Control and Freedom are both such excellent ideas is one of the profound ironies of life. Socialist and Tory, Liberal and Anarchist—both these devoted couples have good cases on paper; and yet the human being in us all is continually tearing them up and filling with them the waste-paper basket. The ills and irregularities of human society seem centred in defects which belong to us irrespective of privilege, party, or politics, and one would as soon expect them to be removed by Socialism, Bolshevism, Fascism, and so forth, as to see fulfilment of the gospel according to Mr. Stone in the novel *Fraternity!* That visionary's thin voice preaching to the night across a shadowy garden is no more the echo of possibility than are the dreams of controlled perfection in the human state. At best, we can but expect ebbings of the tides of inequality, with floods again to follow. This is the height of discouragement if social equality be considered an end in itself. But human happiness is the real end, and equality a somewhat glib and posturing means thereto.

In any case the novelist, if he be an artist, is neither politician nor schoolmaster; he can claim no teacher's temperament and no direct function. His contribution (not inconsiderable) to social and ethical values must be by way of the painting of character and environment. And such painting may take either of two forms—the negative, realistic and quasi-satiric, which stares Character straight in the face, or looks a little down at it, showing what men might be by giving defects due prominence; or the romantic, which stares up at Character, and shows what men might be by painting heroes or earthly paradises, and stressing their virtues and delights. A novelist, like his reader, is disposed by nature to one of these methods or to the other—occasionally to both.

To one who speaks with the partiality of a practitioner, the first method seems the most natural and effective. Most of the great characters of fiction, nearly all those who have contributed to ethical values—Don Quixote, Sancho Panza, Hamlet, Lear, Falstaff, Tom Jones, Faust, d'Artagnan, Sam Weller, Betsy Trotwood, Micawber, Becky Sharp, Major Pendennis, Bel-Ami, Irena, Bazarov, Natasha, Stepan Arcadyevitch, Anna Karenina—have been conceived and painted in that manner. The sophisticated reader does not like being led by the nose, any more than the sophisticated novelist—so far as one may speak for that breed—likes leading him. The intelligent prefer to deduce for themselves rather than to be shown the shining example; for, however it may be in life, in fiction the heroic cloys the palate. We find a clear if crude illustration of that truth in the figure of Athos in Dumas's Musketeer series. In the first part, when he is not fighting he is usually drunk, and we love him. In the second and third parts he has become so noble that the tortuous Aramis, the portentous Porthos usurp his place in our affections. The demand for the perfect or heroic in fiction is, indeed, the cry of such as do not understand the implications of their own request. It is a sure sign of inexperience; and, in general, evidence of a deficient æsthetic sense.

The novelist, then, if he deals with Society, and has anything of the critic in him, will unconsciously be something of a satirist. Telling the truth, as he sees and feels it, he will not subscribe to popular superstitions, however wholesome; and when he is painting Society he cannot avoid treading on corns or holding foibles up to daylight. To him each section of Society, professionals and plutocrats, the squirearchy, the intellectuals, the aristocrats—each will have its weak point, its doom; the negative, so to speak, of its virtues. To illustrate from one's own work: The Forsytes, with all their sound and saving sense, have their exaggerated love of property; the Pendyces of *The Country House* in their pluck a core of crass obstinacy; the Dallisons of *Fraternity* to their cultured sympathy the appendix of fastidious indecision; and the Carádocs of *The Patrician,* though endowed with the sense of duty, decisiveness, and high spirit, are atrophied in their emotional capacity by their inbred love of leadership. But though it is the novelist's part to hold up a mirror so that people see themselves as they are, we may trust the Forsytes, Pendyces, and Carádocs of this life to remain unaware of their special "dooms"; and to carry on, lifting their noses above the satirist and all his works, while the intellectual Dallisons will already have seen their doom before it is shown to them.

What purpose then will the novelist serve? Well! By depicting a section of life in due relation to the whole of life without fear or favour, he does not cure the section, but he does throw it into proper relief for the general eye, and indirectly fosters evolution.

If, on the other hand, his theme is more elemental and he is treating, say, of passion, he can but ill speak truth, walking with his right hand in Mrs. Grundy's and his left hand in Dr. Watts'! And yet to write grossly of sex, to labour in a story the physical side of love is to err æsthetically—to overpaint; for the imagination of readers requires little stimulus in this direction, and the sex impulse is so strong that any emphatic physical description pulls the picture out of perspective. A naïve or fanatical novelist may think that by thoroughly exploring sex he can reform the human attitude to it; but a man might as well enter the bowels of the earth with the intention of coming out on the other side.

If it were not for the physical side of love we should none of us be here, and the least sophisticated of us knows intuitively so much about it that to tell us more, except in scientific treatises, is to carry coals to Newcastle. But the atmosphere and psychology of passion are other matters; and the trackless maze in which the average reader wanders where his feelings are concerned is none the worse for a night-light or two. In every artist, moreover, who is not a freak there is a sensibility to the scent and colour of the dark flower, to its fascination, and the fates lurking within its lure, which demands a vent. And though—especially in England and America—many novelists deliberately stifle this sensibility, and treat of passion exclusively as the prelude to wedding-bells, they do so at the expense of truth and their stature as artists.

The school of thought which would limit a novelist's range of subject to what may desirably be placed in the hands of the young person has been summed up in the figure of Podsnap, and is of course primarily Anglo-American. But such explanation as biologists may offer of the puritanical streak in Anglo-Saxon blood will leave the artist unconsoled and open to the attacks of a particularly virulent type of intolerance, which produces in him a spirit of revolt, often expressing itself in terms of sexual exaggeration equally undesirable. The artist is better advised to pay no attention, but to tell the truth as delicately and decently as he can. *L'excès est toujours un mal,* whether in Puritan or his victim.

The artist, they say, is not concerned with morals, but really no one is more concerned with morals if a long view be taken. For to the artist we look for those pictures of life as it really is, those correlations of sectional life to the whole, essential to the organic moral growth of human society. Moralists, preachers, judges, business men are all by nature or occupation advocates of the *status quo;* radicals and reformers are all professional partisans of the millennium. Yet history tells us that the *status quo* is of all things most liable to depart, the millennium of all things least likely to arrive; and the artist, alone steering clear of *parti pris,* furnishes the light by which the path of—if not progress—at least development can be discerned.

Conversion of others to his own way of thinking, however, is certainly no direct part of a novelist's business. Let him think and let think. When he has so selected and arranged his material as to drive home the essential significance of his theme, and pressed out from human nature the last ounce of its resistance to Fate, he has done his job; in so doing, however, he will often seem to be exploiting some social problem, or grinding the axe of a reform, when he has really only selected circumstances and environment which will most surely and suitably bring out the fundamental qualities of his characters.

The emotional, social, or political extravagances of society pass the skill of doctors, and their redress must be left to Nature, who—generally at the eleventh hour—administers a purge so drastic that it kills or cures. The world has an incurable habit of going on, with possibly a tendency towards improvement in human life; and the novelist, like any other specimen of mankind, fits into the slow pattern, and cannot flatter himself that he is directly altering the regulator or accelerating the pulses of the clock. His influence, sometimes a very real if subtle influence, is confined to a mental quickening, to a species of spiritual infection from his positively or negatively expressed passion. All he can do is to present truth as he sees it, and, gripping with it his readers, produce in them a sort of mental and moral ferment, whereby vision may be encouraged, imagination enlivened, and understanding promoted. And always he must expect to be mistaken and to be criticised.

Of art as a whole it is safe to say that the critic should be ready to accept the theme and the medium selected by the artist, and having accepted, should then criticise the work for being, or not being, what it is meant to be. But this counsel of perfection is not often followed even by critics who would admit its truth. In going our own ways we novelists will be charged with many opposite faults of temperament and texture, and if we are impressionable will stop writing out of sheer bewilderment. We shall be rated for pessimism and for idealism; for soulless impartiality and for sentimentality; for chilly artistry and for rash propagandism; for barren cleverness and for naïve humanitarianism; for bitterness and for sweetness; for lack of vision and for being visionary; and often, perhaps, with justice. But the fact is that a self-consciousness which checks or heats our moods in response to criticism reduces us to impotence. Better that we take ourselves as the tides of our being dictate, and let ourselves go upon them; for, after all, we do not choose our subjects—it is they who choose us. Life forces itself on us and gives us no rest until it has secured expression and received thereby quietus. But in going our own ways let it be *aequo animo,* laying no flattering unction to our souls.

The beauty of the world is the novelist's real despair; the heartache that he feels in the presence of Nature in flower. Maybe that ache is part of the sex instinct—a longing for fusion or union with beauty beheld; or, more rudely, might be called greed—the desire for the perpetual and intimate possession of loveliness. The effort to paint or render that loveliness in words is, then, a natural resort, an attempt to slake longing, which achieves, alas! but the mere shadow of fulfilment.

Truth and beauty are a hard quest, but what else is there worth seeking? Absorption in that quest brings to the novelist his reward—unconsciousness of self, and the feeling that he plays his part as best he may. At the back of all work, even a novelist's, lies some sort of philosophy. And if the novelist now writing may for a moment let fall the veil from the face of his own, he will confess: That human realisation of a First Cause is to him inconceivable. He is left to acceptance of what is. Out of Mystery

we came, into Mystery return. Life and death, ebb
and flow, day and night, world without beginning
and without end is all that he can grasp. But in such
little certainty he sees no cause for gloom. Life for
those who still have vital instinct in them is good
enough in itself, even if it lead to nothing further;
and we humans have only ourselves to blame if we
alone, among the animals, so live that we lose the
love of life for itself. And as for the parts we play,
courage and kindness seem the elemental virtues,
for they include all that is real in any of the others,
alone make human life worth while, and bring an
inner happiness.

1926.

FOUR MORE NOVELISTS IN PROFILE

PROFILE

AN ADDRESS

FOUR MORE NOVELISTS IN
PROFILE

A WRITER, who is not one of those celestial beings, professional critics, does not talk of other writers unless he has a passion for them. Now a living writer very seldom has a passion for other living writers; on the contrary, he is generally in a passion about them; so the four writers that I am going to talk about are all dead. It is the only thing they have in common. They are a band divorced by aim and temperament—as far apart as four next door neighbours in a London street, or four doctors diagnosing a disease.

I began to read Dumas when I was twenty-five, a callow youth upon my travels. I began with "Monte Cristo," and I read it on the sailing ship "Torrens" crossing the Indian Ocean; with the royals and stunsails of my mind set, I traversed the phantasmagorian immensity of this tale. I remember that, in the Doldrums, I would take my green-tinged volume out on to the bowsprit away from those mere creatures of reality—my fellow passengers. Alone with romance and flying fish, I read and read. For the next four years, like some grave toper, I soaked myself in Dumas—not the syndicate of that name, but the writer of "The Musketeer" books, and "The Reine Margot" books. I also sipped at "Joseph Balsamo," and "Le Collier de la Reine"; but a sip was enough, and into the rest of the ninety or so novels I have not dipped. Still, "Monte Cristo" and those two series—"The Musketeer" and "The Reine Margot" —contain a little matter of twenty-five volumes, which is enough to swear by. To maturer judgment "Monte Cristo" lags even further behind the "Reine Margot" series than that series lags behind the great "Musketeer" trilogy which definitely places Dumas at the head of all the writers of historical romance. His power, indeed, of creating history is almost disastrous. History according to Dumas is so much more real than history according to historians, that those poor fellows have never had a chance since. They might tell you that this or that was so, such and such personages of such and such complexion, but, having read Dumas, you knew better. He ran amok in the streets of the Past, and left behind him the pallid corpses of historians. Sedulous truth wanders like a disinherited ghost among his rich fables. Who can read historically of Richelieu, or Mazarin, of Charles IX, Anne of Austria, Louise de la Vallière, Le Grand Monarque, Les Ducs de Guise, et d'Anjou, Henri of Navarre and La Reine Margot, when he has gone to school with them at l'école Dumas? I went to school with the late Prime Minister, and when I used to read of him on the heights of Olympus, I merely thought of one who wiped my eye at Horace or whose too-too-solid shins encountered my boots on the football field. I doubted the reality of his later activities. Just so is it doubtful whether France had any history outside the pages of Dumas.

It has been the mode of late for writers to take some historical personage and make him or her the centre of a biographical play or novel: if you desire to measure Dumas' genius, line these modern recreations up beside the Frenchman's historical figures, and you will find the moderns pale and thin, lacking in flavour and fascination. And then make another comparison: line up Dumas' historical characters with the figures of his fancy, such as D'Artagnan, Aramis, Porthos, Athos, Coconnas, Chicot, Bussy (who though they had their living prototypes never paid any attention to them) and his genius will be still more apparent, for these figures of his unfettered imagination are even more vigorous and alive than his historical characters. Dumas excelled with men rather than with women. Anne of Austria, Margot, Louise, la dame de Monsoreau, and la Duchesse de Chévreuse, are good but not great creations; Miladi is a mere monstress, and no other of his women are terribly exciting. But his male figures ruffle it with the very best; they simply strut through Time—'rich,' our fathers would have called them! While for zest in narrative Dumas is the equal of Dickens, and more than that one cannot say. Sniff if you like at his "panache," as at the extravagance of the English master, but that which offends in lesser writers seems natural to the make-up of these great showmen.

I must apologize for mentioning narrative in days

when so many regard it as a dead and buried form
and are engaged in trying to express the human
story by a series of hyphenated detonations; but
really one cannot leave it out in speaking of Dumas.
At his best he had no peer at sustaining the interest
of a tale. He generally had a number of plots, and
drove them four-in-hand at a sharp and steady pace
and with a fine evenness of motion. "Le Vicomte de
Bragelonne" is, perhaps, for wealth of incident and
character intricately interwoven, his greatest effort.
Oh! Undoubtedly a great raconteur! And with something of the magician about him, but a magician who
used the pigments and potions of actual life and feeling. Highly-coloured and strongly-flavoured Dumas
was, but he was never windy and just fanciful.

Fiction from the days of Homer on has been devised to satisfy two demands—for narrative and for
character. Human nature changes so slowly that a
thousand years are but as yesterday; and the reader
requires narrative and character to-day just as much
as he did in the time of Chaucer. Dumas, though he
may be scouted by the eclectic, is still read eagerly,
and will be read a hundred, nay, three hundred years
on. While nothing, I think, is more certain than that
no single work of what one may call protoplasmic
fiction—spineless, all jelly and wriggles—will be remembered even by name thirty years hence.

The line of distinction between realism and romance lies in the paramount mood of the writer; so
that he who is bent primarily on entertaining is a
romanticist. and he who is bent primarily on reveal-

ing, or if you like interpreting, is a realist. I have
said that before, but my experience tells me that
what you have said before you had better say again,
if you want anybody to pay attention to it. Dumas
then must be accounted a romanticist, for he is bent
primarily on entertaining. His work gives practically
no indication that he had predilections, prejudices,
passions or philosophy. His tales offer no criticism
of life, are written from no temperamental angle.
Of English writers perhaps only Shakespeare is so
completely impersonal. But though he was a romanticist, he never got into the air. Romantic in mood,
he was realistic in method, and he had his absorp-
tions in character.

His greatest creation is undoubtedly D'Artagnan,
that backbone of eleven volumes, type at once of the
fighting adventurer and of the trusty servant, whose
wily blade is ever at the back of those whose hearts
have neither his magnanimity nor his courage, but
whose heads have a cold concentration that his head
lacks. Few, if any, characters in fiction inspire one
with such belief in their individual existences, or
their importance as types. D'Artagnan is the world's
'lieutenant'—the man who does the job that others
profit by; and he is none the less fascinating because
he is always "going to make his fortune" out of it,
and never does anything but make someone else's.
So very like such a lot of people! To one who made
D'Artagnan all shall be forgiven.

With seven-leagued boots one leaps from Dumas

to the Russian Tchehov, more modern than the moderns. Now, of Tchehov I would say that his stories have apparently neither head nor tail, they seem to be all middle like a tortoise. Many who have tried to imitate him however have failed to realise that the heads and tails are only tucked in. Just as one cannot see or paint like Whistler by merely wishing to, so one cannot feel or write like Tchehov because one thinks his is a nice new way. One young modern writer, Katharine Mansfield, has proved a definite exception to a fairly general rule of failure, not, indeed, because she was a better copyist than the others, but because she had the same intense and melancholy emotionalism as Tchehov, the same way of thinking and feeling, and died—alas!—of the same dread malady. I should say that Tchehov has been the most potent magnet to young writers in several countries for the last twenty years. He was a very great writer, but his influence has been almost wholly dissolvent. For he worked naturally in a method which seems easy, but which is very hard for Westerners, and his works became accessible to Western Europe at a time when writers were restless, and eager to make good without hard labour— a state of mind not so confined to writers that it cannot be noticed also among plumbers, and on the Stock Exchange.

Tchehov appeared to be that desirable thing, the "short cut," and it is hardly too much to say that most of those who have taken him have never arrived. His work has been a will-o'-the-wisp. Writers may think they have just to put down faithfully the daily run of feeling and event, and they will have a story as marvellous as those of Tchehov. Alas! things are not made 'marvellous' by being called so, or there would be a good many 'marvellous' things to-day. It is much harder for a Westerner than for a Russian to dispense with architecture in the building of a tale, but a good many Western writers now appear to think otherwise.

I don't wish to convey the impression of insensibility to the efforts and achievements of our 'new' fiction; which has so out-Tchehoved Tchehov that it doesn't know its own father. Very able and earnest writers are genuinely endeavouring with astounding skill to render life in its kaleidoscopic and vibrational aspects; they are imbued too with a kind of pitiful and ironic fatalism which seems to them new perhaps, but which is eminently Tchehovian, and can be found also in the work of many other writers whom they affect to have outgrown. There is that which is genuinely new in the style and methods of some of these adventuring new fictionists, but I do not think there is anything new in their philosophy of life. They have thrown over story and character, or rather the set and dramatic ways of depicting story and character; but they are no more philosophically emancipated than their forebears, Turgenev, De Maupassant, Flaubert, Henry James, Meredith, Hardy, France, Conrad. The kind of mysticism which these new writers claim as their own brand is no more mystical than that which lies at the back of the work of any of these older writers, all of whom have given ample evidence of recognising the mysterious and sufficing rhythm of creation, and the beauty, terror, pity and irony with which human life is shot through and through. The style and method in fact of these new "fictionists" are more arresting than their philosophy. I admire their adventurous industry even if it is a little too self-conscious; but I cannot help wondering whether in their clever daring wholesale dismissal of shape and selected sequence they have not missed the truth that human lives, for all their appearance of volatility in these days of swift motion, are really tethered to deep and special roots. Now in his tales, unshaped though they seem, Tchehov never forgot that truth, nor is he ever over-sophisticated.

He was born in 1860 at Taganrog in Russia and died in the Black Forest aged only forty-four. He came of peasant stock and followed the calling of a country doctor. There is no other of the older Russian writers with such an understanding of the Russian mind and the Russian heart, or such an intuitive sense of the typical Russian nature. He seemed to brood over its temperamental bonelessness as over a doom; and his work is one long objective revelation of it. A country doctor sees more of human nature than most men, he sees it under the harrow of pain and misadventure, and stripped of all aid except 'character.' It must have been a nightmare to Tchehov, a man of great sensibility, and some method, to watch his fellow-creatures in their troubles, hopelessly unaided by their national temperament, of which, with the detachment of a born artist, he was keenly conscious. The Russian temperament, to speak rashly as if it were a single thing in a country containing many races, lays practically no store by time or place; it excels in feeling, still more perhaps in the expression of feeling, so that its aims are washed out by fresh tides of feeling before they can be achieved. The Russian temperament, in many ways very attractive, seems incapable of halting on a mark. That is why it has always been, and I think will always be, the prey of a bureaucracy. The Russian temperament flows and ebbs incessantly, the national catchword 'Nichevo'—'it doesn't matter'—expresses well the fatalism of its perpetual flux. Material things and the principles which they connote, do not matter enough to the Russian nature, emotion and its current expression matter too much. That is speaking, of course, from the English point of view. A Russian would say that to us material things and the principles they connote, matter too much; emotion and its expression too little. Well, it is just this contrast between national temperaments which makes the Tchehovian form so attractive to and so unsuitable for English writers. That form is flat as the plains of his country. And Tchehov's triumph was that he made flatness exciting, as exciting as a prairie or a desert is to those who first encounter it. How he did this was a secret, which many since have supposed they understood, but which, speaking bluntly, they have not.

His plays, too, are never adequately performed on the English stage. Partly because they are written for Russian actors who are perhaps the best in the world; partly because of his method and temperament. English actors cannot render the atmosphere of a Tchehov play. But it is just the atmosphere—whether of play or story—which makes the work of Tchehov memorable.

Intuitive knowledge of human emotions gives to his stories a spiritual shape, which takes the place of the shape supplied by dramatic event. He never wrote a full-length novel, probably because the longer your story, the greater the need for something definite to happen. As for his characters, they are either too true to life or perhaps merely too Russian to be remembered by name. One recalls the figures in 'The Cherry Orchard' or in 'Uncle Vanya' —I can even clap a name to one or two—as very living, very actual, but so under the shadow of mood and of atmosphere, that they haunt the corridors rather than take their seats in the assembly house. Still, there is transcendent merit in Tchehov's writings, for he reveals to us the very soul of a great people, and that with a minimum of parade or pretence.

If with seven-leagued boots one leaps from Dumas to Tchehov, then with ten-leagued boots one springs from Tchehov to Stevenson. So far as Art can ever be depressing, there is perhaps no more depressing writer than Tchehov; he is just as emphatically an author from whom we turn away when our sands run low, as the Scotsman Stevenson is *the* writer whose books we take up if we have influenza. I wonder, by the way, if you have noticed that tragic writers are generally blessed with very good health. We must not count the Russians because they always express what they really feel; but we Westerners naturally put up a fight against our feelings. If we feel bad we become humorists or at least take to romancing. If he had been gifted with good health Stevenson might have been a great tragic writer; as it was he simply had to be lighthearted. He escaped into ink, and was never so happy as with a drawn pen in his hand. The older I get, the more I appreciate him. Which some would say is a sign of dotage. I used to say it myself in the days of my youth. For at that time I was so given to sitting in the French and Russian draughts that were blowing in the then rather stuffy room of English fiction, and so, as they say, 'fed-up' with the undiscriminating Stevensonian chorus of that period, that I used to look on him as an 'agreeable rattle' rather mannered and incurably romantic. I know better now. True! He is not a main-stream *novelist;* he had not health enough to spare for any great philosophic urge or any very robust curiosity. He lived, too, in the moment, and to the full—not of the type which psychologises and worries about whys and wherefores. But he is a main-stream *writer,* and what I used to take for acquired 'manner' I now feel to be the natural expression of an intensely vivid, sensitised and adventurous spirit. His style, with its unexpectedness of diction, in almost every sentence, must be acquitted of exoticism or the smell of the lamp. It expressed a curiously glancing nature, a continually stimulated interest, and it was munitioned quite naturally by startling powers of observation and a superb memory. I open a book of his at random, and the first sentence I read is this: "High rocky hills, as blue as sapphire, closed the view, and between these lay ridge upon ridge, heathery, craggy, the sun glittering on veins of rock, the underwood *clambering* in the hollows, as *rude* as God made them *at the first.*"

"Clambering"—"rude"—"at the first." Now I don't think Stevenson had to hunt for those three expressions, which give the valued spring of unexpectedness to that somewhat ordinary sentence. I think they just jumped into his mind. Indeed, always excepting Shakespeare—and perhaps Mr. Wodehouse—I doubt if any other British writer has used the unexpected with more apt spontaneity. Whatever commentators may say on this point, that has become my conviction from re-reading him; and it is an attribute so priceless as to make up for multitudinous deficiencies. Unlike many stylists so-called, Stevenson is very easy to read, sentence by sentence; the unexpected words call no halt, and the grammar is clear as good spring water—no heavy-footed rounding-up, no violent ellipses, no attempts to get effect by vain and damnable iteration.

Stevenson, like Dumas, was a romanticist; absorbed in telling a tale rather than revealing human types and phases of human life. In 'Kidnapped' and 'Catriona,' truly, he was not far off being absorbed equally in tale and character, which is the happy mean; and, again, at the end of his life he was trying for realism in 'The Ebb Tide' and 'Weir of Hermiston.' But in the round he was a romanticist. As Andrew Lang observes, in his preface to the Swanston edition, he "never sought his subjects in the main stream of contemporary life, or made an attempt to interpret existence, as they knew it, to his readers." All through Stevenson's writings one is conscious of a questing and adventurous nature, incurably gallant in the practical affairs of life; introspective without morbidity, with a certain dread, indeed, of going too deeply into things. His chief fault, as novelist, was taking themes scarcely worthy of his powers. Where, as in 'Dr. Jekyll and Mr. Hyde,' his subject is deep, he shies at it, and the result is somewhat lurid. In 'The Ebb Tide' he is almost alarmed by his own lack of compromise in handling what our critics are so fond of calling the 'sordid' side of life. How he would have ended 'Weir of Hermiston' it is difficult to say—but he would probably have run away from the tragic story planned, although, if you remember, his lovers were to end happily, or, rather, in America.

As a teller of a tale, though in a slighter way, he is the equal of Dumas and Dickens; and he is their superior in dexterity and swiftness. There are no *longueurs* in Stevenson. He had but one main theme, that essential theme of romance, the struggle between the good and the bad, of hero against villain, and often with the heroine absent, or merely looking over the wall. For there was an eternal boy in Stevenson, and he wrote 'Virginibus Puerisque.'

Of his novels—'Kidnapped' and 'Catriona,' taken together, come easily first. In this work, besides all the allure of a fine tale, there is most admirable type-drawing. Alan Breck and David Balfour may well stand for the highlands and the lowlands for all time; while in Catriona and Barbara Grant he has drawn his two best female characters. But, beyond all this, there is in that particular work a sublimation of his love for Scotland, a breath of heather and the sea, a pride of country, and an atmosphere of home such as few books exhale. I put 'The Master of Ballantrae' second. This book survives the ever-handicapping method of narration in the first person extremely well, and the Master himself is a notable rascal. I have a weakness for that stirring tale 'The Black Arrow,' which gives a livelier picture of mediæval times than I remember elsewhere in fiction. 'Treasure Island,' of course, stands by itself as a pure yarn. 'The Wrecker' and 'The Ebb Tide' are rather out of drawing, as books by two hands tend to be, but I at least re-read them with pleasure. 'St. Ives' is one of those capital stories that one can never remember and so can always read again; it would have been better left unfinished. 'The Wrong Box' is great fun. I could have done without 'Dr. Jekyll and Mr. Hyde,' the least Stevensonian book he ever wrote, but that which, owing to the public's native perversity, first brought him popular attention, and, as I read the other day, is still looked-on as his high-water mark. As for 'Weir of Hermiston,' I do not subscribe to Sir Sydney Colvin's opinion, which is shared by many, that it promised to be Stevenson's best work of fiction. It is interesting, because it was a decided attempt to break with the romantic; but it discloses rather fatally the weakness of Stevenson when he tries to give you the real inside of human beings. Archie is a failure, and Christine seems to me on the way to becoming one.

Stevenson was so vivid and attractive as a person, so picturesque in his travels and his ways of life, so copious and entrancing in his essays and his letters, and so pleasing as a poet, that his general self overshadows him as novelist. But compare with his novels all the romantic novels written since, even those heavenly twins 'The Prisoner of Zenda,' and 'Rupert of Hentzau,' and you will see how high he stands. In fact, next to Dumas, he is the best of all the romantic novelists, certainly the best British romanticist, and I shall be extremely astonished if at this time of day he is ever deposed from that position. For though the world is not yet too old to read and enjoy romance, it grows less and less capable, I think, of producing writers with the bloom that Stevenson had on his spirit, and the spring he had in the heels of his fancy. I suppose there is nothing to prevent us moderns from dipping our pens in fancy. But, since Dumas and Stevenson wrote, something has happened. Tune has gone out of the world.

Romanticists to-day can turn out quite good tales
of tubs with bodies inside them, and that kind of
thing; but those who try to ride Pegasus—such as
John Masefield in his 'Sard Harker' vein, or John
Buchan—are a bit too conscious of the creature's
wings. Romance may bring up the 9.15, but it brings
it up full of business men from Chislehurst or Croy-
don. Aeroplanes and limousines buzz in all our bonnets. Machines have crept into the writing of
romance, and when machines clatter in the brain, we
hear no longer the piping on the hills. And so, I think,
we shall not see Stevenson dethroned. And I am
fairly certain that, of British nineteenth century
writers, he will live longer than any except Dickens.

Though W. H. Hudson is best known as an observer and lover of Nature, he shall be spoken of
here only as a novelist—the author of 'The Purple
Land,' 'El Ombu' and 'Green Mansions,' each a
masterpiece in its very different way. Hudson was
a genius, but I will not suggest that he was a creative genius led away and destroyed by a vamp called
Nature. He quite probably had no more fiction in
him than actually came out of him, for one may
fairly say that writers produce what they must.
Hudson scored a bull's-eye, however, with each of
those three books. In 'The Purple Land' he wrote
the best Picaresque novel in English of the last
hundred and more years; in 'El Ombu' he gave us
an example of simple and tragic recital hard to beat;
and in 'Green Mansions' he left behind him quite

the rarest fantasy of our times. As a writer of fiction he was completely original, unfettered, and unaffected. Of no school, uninfluenced by any previous master, he blew-in to the world of the novel on a wind as free as the air of the Pampas where he was born, or one of those Cornish gales he loved to be out in. 'The Purple Land,' written, I think, in the eighties of the last century, if not earlier, is the record of a young man's wandering adventures in the Argentine of old days. It has probably some semi-biographical foundation, or at least drops here and there into the truth of reminiscence—some of its episodes are tinged with the glamour of private enjoyment; the author has plagiarised certain sensations of his own. If Dicky Lamb, the hero poursuivant, cannot be taken for Hudson himself, he was evidently intimate with the adventures and acquaintances of Hudson's own youth. The essence of the Picaresque novel is zest in arriving at fresh places, and seeing new faces, mostly female; and this is certainly the essence of 'The Purple Land.' It is the work of a man in love with living, so it has never been very popular. Most people are not in love with living; they don't shoot life on the wing, they pot at it sitting, after having carefully ascertained it to be eatable. We don't like random adventures that lead us nowhere; we belong to an age whose strong suit is insurance. 'The Purple Land' is told of another world in days when insurance was unknown and men rode forth to love or fight. Besides the book has a Spanish savour, which accounts for the mod-

erate transports with which English-speaking people
have received it. After all, we want morals not man-
dolins.

'El Ombu,' the chief tale of Hudson's second work
of fiction, is elemental and tragic enough; but I
would not rank it with Turgenev's 'Lear of the
Steppes,' and 'Torrents of Spring'; nor with Conrad's 'Youth,' 'Heart of Darkness' and 'Typhoon';
nor with Mérimée's 'Carmen,' Maupassant's 'Boule
de Suif,' Flaubert's 'Cœur Simple,' nor Mr. Mau-
gham's 'Rain'—stories of like length—all elemental,
and with the exception of 'Youth' and 'Typhoon,'
tragic in their nature; 'El Ombu,' though it centres
loosely round the great tree which gives it name,
has neither the backbone nor the inevitability of
those other great tales. This disjointed narrative of
unrelieved disaster, told by an old shepherd of the
plains in wild days, is a set of variations, as it were,
on the violence of human passions. But its noble
simplicity of language, and its atmosphere make it
an impressive piece of work. Like 'The Purple
Land,' it is probably rooted in fact; woven out of
folk lore of the Pampas in days starker and more
violent than they now are. Plains, by the way, are
to Hudson's writings what the sea was to Conrad's,
except that by Hudson Nature is loved, by Conrad
dreaded. Compare, for instance, the forest in Conrad's 'Heart of Darkness' and the forest in Hudson's
'Green Mansions'; the first is a monstrous gloomy
threat, the second a wild and lovely refuge.

'Green Mansions,' the third of Hudson's title

deeds to fame as novelist, is a book so apart, so amazingly unlike the usual run of fiction, that I missed its beauty on a first reading. I came to appreciate it on a second perusal ten years later. It is the only book I know which has really succeeded in welding woodnotes wild into a tune. Rima, the bird girl of the forest, embodies at once the spell of Nature, and the yearning of the human soul for that intimacy with Nature which through self-consciousness—or shall we say town-life—we have lost. She stands alone in literature for immaterial beauty. I recoil from the much-debated statue of Rima set up three years ago in Hyde Park. The task was impossible, indeed, for any artist, however original. Metal and stone are unsuited to the volatile and rarefied. In the figure of Rima Hudson was trying to express the uncanny sympathy with all that is not human, and especially with the winged and sweet-songed freedom of birds, which he beyond all men felt. And to see it travestied by this self-confident and massive product of a studio is, to one who knew Hudson, a kind of desecration. Such things are done in haste—repented of at leisure. Hudson the novelist is certainly dwarfed, for those who knew him, by Hudson the man; for he was the rarest, the most unique, personality of his time, the one whose understanding stepped furthest out of the merely human ring, the one who succeeded best to see the face of Nature as it is. In him, wise and cultured though he was, there was yet something of primitive man, something even of the beasts and birds he loved.

Still, if he had left behind him no personal impress, nor any nature writings, but just these three pieces of fiction, he must yet have been accounted a rare and potent figure.

Editors sometimes ask what the future of the novel is going to be. It is a question no one can answer. The future of the novel does not depend on this or that fashion in technique, or such and such economic developments, it depends on whether or no accident is going to throw up novelists endowed with one or other, or preferably both, of two qualities neither of which can be defined. These qualities are Stature and Charm. By the law of averages each decade should provide about the same number of novelists so endowed; but study of the Past will disclose, I think, considerable gaps; and study of the Present will cause some uneasiness in regard to the Future. There is something about this Age which is inimical to Stature. Even individual temperament is being levelled down by publicity, limelight, standardisation, specialisation, and rapid communications. It seems curious, but I think it is true, that the intellectual activity we call cleverness is inimical to Stature—and this is a very clever Age, and getting cleverer. Charm is not so much endangered, perhaps, but it is in danger enough. For Charm is a nooky quality, and the nook is getting rare. The settled, homespun, or at least home-scented, existence which used to lay its mark on the spirits of men and women, and give a loved or hated background to their thoughts, is daily being 'improved' away. Art that can stand up above the waters of life, or that can smile apart, or that can do both, is rooted in deep and quiet things, in private and fervent feelings. And I will leave you to judge how far the times are inclined to let us call our souls our own.

Well, it is because of charm and stature, one or both, that we turn to books a second and third time. And only those books to which we can turn again have any chance of living on. Of the making of books there is no end, of the talking about them still less end, and I will wind up with a remark or two about the talkers, including myself. The permanent reputation of a writer, or of a book, cannot be made by talking about it. During the thirty odd years since I began to write, I have known dozens of books, talked of as if they were going to be the last word in permanence, by now as dead as if they had never been. The unseen motion of Time's fan drifts to the winds all that has not the magic stuff 'life' in it. An ironical recorder, keeping entry of tongue-made reputations and their duration, would have indeed a curious notion of our critical taste. And I will say to myself and all those others who blow the bubble of reputation from mouth to mouth: Back your taste, by all means, but remember that by all the evidence of history, it is probably bad!

1928.

LITERATURE AND LIFE

AN ADDRESS

LITERATURE AND LIFE

How are we to define Literature? Writers, of course, are better dead before we talk about them, so we will assume that nothing is literature until its perpetrator is no more; but even then we are faced with an infinity of works and an ever-changing opinion about them. I cannot, indeed, imagine any two persons in this hall agreeing for more than two minutes on what is Literature and what is not. Perhaps we would all admit Shakespeare. But apart from Shakespeare, how are we to select? You see, it is not as if we marked our poets as we mark our eggs, "new-laid," so that they may always remain fresh in spite of the lapse of time. No, we allow them to date themselves.

I have a personal prejudice, wholly unreasonable, towards regarding nothing as literature unless I can read it. That cuts out quite a number of great names. But apart from individual taste, to assess Literature is to be like a manager trying to choose for his theatre what the Public wants, except that he has to make his choice before the Public has wanted, and we make ours after—and what a comfort that is! But then—alas!—unlike the manager's Public which is that of to-day—ours is the Public of generation after generation. 1600 laps up what 1800 cannot away with, 1830 makes a name and 1930 scores it through.

Literature, in fact, leaves her footsteps not on the sands but on the quicksands of Time, and I am sorry for the detective who has to find the body from those footsteps. So I think we will give definition a miss. I was, however, talking to a writer friend the other day who was making a serious attempt, by reading old plays, to discover what it is that really makes a literary work last. He had come to the conclusion that it was vitality in the characters. And he was not far wrong, I think, in so far as plays and novels are concerned; but even then one must find something else to cover poetry. And probably it comes to this: A work to be Literature (with the large L) must have genuine individuality of its own. It must be essentially unlike what has gone before.

Did you ever see the skeleton of a snake—one of the most delicate and amazing things in the world? Well, Literature might be compared with the skeleton of a never-ending snake, each vertebra subtly distinct from the next, and miraculously conjoined to it. Or let me take another illustration from natural history. A few years ago in New York I saw a Diplodoccus; an enormous reptile with a vast carcass, an extravagant tail and a tiny mouth; not a live Diplodoccus—though one meets creatures almost as remarkable, and with even smaller mouths. I said to the professor who was taking us round:

274

"Professor, how on earth could such a vast creature have nourished itself with a mouth that size?" He looked at me "kunedon," as if to say: "You have said what I ought to have said first." But the point is that Literature is a kind of Diplodoccus with a huge carcass, a tail you can never get to the end of, and a tiny mouth, always nibbling at Life. I use that word (before I come to it, so to speak) knowing very well that some people think that Literature should not be on speaking terms with Life, that it should just bow distantly and precede Life in to dinner. And that other people think that Literature should be more lively than Life itself, and jazz along without fussing about sequence, selection or shape, or drawing from Life any sort of moral—if I may use that vulgar word; that Literature, in fact, should be what is called a behaviorist, like the ultra-modern music which sits down to compose with the prayer: "O God! let me not drop into a tune!" I know all that, but I am incurably old-fashioned, and for me Literature only comes into being at all when Life strikes sparks out of a temperament—not the sort of Life that strikes sparks out of the policeman and the newspaper, no—the whole vast, restless, rumorous pageant with its glow and its scent, its depth and its darkness, of which each of us is a little separate manifestation, and of which all the rest acts and reacts on each of us in a different way. It is when that action and reaction is vivid enough that there start forth from some lucky one of us visions chiselled in words; and Literature is born. That little new shining vertebra—at first perhaps unrecognized—in time shakes into its place in the unending skeleton of Literature. Literature is a chain of new gems, no two alike. Emphatically, Literature has a spine; I am a firm believer in the spine, and have a horror of contortionism. If we look back into the past we readily discern the backbone of Literature's development. And they who try to snap the spine of Literature and start afresh, only waste their own time and that of those who watch their contortions.

Whatever interesting experiments, for instance, may be made to turn the novel into a kaleidoscope of life after some young novelists; into a domestic encyclopædia after Proust; into a Catherine wheel of sensation after Edgar Wallace; or a treatise on psychoanalytic bacteriology after I won't say who —I feel sure that thirty years hence we shall see all these experiments forgotten and that the only surviving novels will be those with character and story.

Of poetry, I am equally sure, only that will live which either by its content or its rhythm, in some mysterious way stirs our emotions. I dare not say what I should like to say about painting, for painters, in my experience, are even more touchy than literary men. Shall I ever forget the agitation of a connoisseur in a Berlin picture gallery because I could not wholly agree with him that a certain rhythmical conglomeration of postage stamps, chalk marks, nails, and old bus tickets which was hanging there, was not a more moving picture than the Sis-

tine Madonna? And, as to music, wild horses will
not drag from me the assertion that thirty years
hence human nature will still hanker after melody
and will have forgotten all those confections of
farmyard or factory sounds which appear so fascinating to their confectioners. Nay! I will not even
whisper to you my suspicion that saxophones will
by then have joined those jazz instruments of the
past—the sackbut, psaltery and dulcimer—and only
be found in museums where they cannot be played
on without infringing a law which has become part
of the Constitution.

You may think from all this that I am a confirmed
reactionary who deprecates experiment. Not at all!
Experiment in the arts, as in science, is necessary; it
helps development and has its occasional flower. But
there is this peculiar truth about it. Only one who
experiments out of the sheer necessities of his theme
will create that which will last. They who experiment
from a mere craving for novelty, capture for a season the intelligence of the weaker brethren, and attract the butterflies of the day; but their works fade
like dew off grass when the sun shines—or, to be
more in the vein of modern poetry, salve off the lips
of a young lady under the osculatory process.

Some fifteen years ago in London there was an
exhibition of the works of a certain sculptor, which
contained many sane and admirable pieces. Two
young ladies came in one day, and flitted from flower
to flower with a dissatisfied air, till at last one of
them caught sight of a vast seated assemblage of

elliptical rhomboids which was wooing the Public under the name of Venus. Before this supreme novelty she halted, if a butterfly can halt. "Oh, my dear," she said, "here she is! Here's the Venus!" And putting her head on one side, she added: "Isn't she a pet?" Such butterflies still exist and halt before the works of novelty for novelty's sake, because they are told to by some town-crier, who must have novelty at any cost.

But coming back to Literature: This is, of course, an exceedingly experimental period. So much so, that we writers live in difficult days. Whether poetry is not now prose and prose poetry, is perhaps the least of our doubts. And whether under those circumstances either of them is worth writing, is perhaps the greatest. We seem ready to welcome anything nowadays, and to welcome it with acclamation. Books come out with a bang and have the greatest difficulty in surviving their publishers' advertisements. Scarcely a book escapes being called "great." Masterpieces, and works of genius, are common as gooseberries, and as readily made into jam. Some day, but not in our day, publishers and reviewers will learn that 'Greatness' and 'Genius' are words better left to the assessments of that cold and searching arbiter, Time, who is uncommonly like an income tax collector, not very long to put off by false returns. There is, of course, one advantage about all this drum-beating; books get immediate recognition. That is a good thing, though rather dangerous to young writers. In the old days if a new writer was praised by the cognoscenti, as the early Meredith, or Conrad, or Stephen Crane, were praised, it was almost certain that he wouldn't sell. Now if he is so praised, he goes at once into fifteen editions, is asked by the Press to express his opinion on Prohibition, the Man Mountain, Birth Control and other world-shaking matters, and if his head is not strong—he, or generally she, is soon standing on it.

That is why, I suppose, we writers are regarded by the bulk of our fellow-citizens as being somewhat loose in the top storey. People buy us, but they go about saying: "Oh! yes, literary!" as if convinced that we have got our values wrong. And a good many of us have; which is unfortunate, because a writer's business is to get values at least averagely right, to see keenly, to feel and think deeply, and to express more clearly than other people what we see and feel and think. To be worth our salt we have to be patient; to keep our sense of humour and proportion; to preserve a certain humility, a proper independence, and a real zest.

There are, to-day, any amount of good young writers. I doubt if the power of expression has ever been so high. And the question is not one of talent or of technical accomplishment; the question is one of keeping the head; of having in the heart that which is worth expressing; and of not being deflected by the childish desire to shock, or led off into the backwaters of mere cleverness and pattern-weaving.

And before I pass on to talk about Life, I should like to suggest a thought. The course of any art, painting, music, literature, is a pilgrimage. To what shrine? To see whose face does the artist, bearing his gift, trail across the thirsty sands—the face of beauty; the face of truth; or, only the face of a dancing faun, or of a golden calf? What is the aim and end of our arts? It is time that round our camp-fires we re-asked ourselves that question. There have been decades when the answer has seemed plain; but this is not one of them. We are beset by mirages. They glitter, shift, are gone. And that is not well. For the artist, be he musician, painter, sculptor, writer, is the child of a long line of true believers, who held high their heads, and marched with their eyes on the star. For us, nowadays, the star dances, or flits flaring through the sky, and sometimes there seems no star out. And yet, is there one of us who, when the pipe has been smoked, the talk is spent, the camp-fire dies, does not know the answer and see the star? To that question: Unto what end do we ply our arts, is there any true answer but this?

For the greater grace and dignity of man.

And now concerning Life. No need to worry about a definition there. We shall all agree that it is the great adventure.

We take our tickets for the Unknown Station but once; only once travel through the countryside called Life, and what we do on the way, how we live through that long or short journey, depends on the general temper of our spirits.

I suppose that many think we live in a cheap and sensational age, all sky-signs and headlines; an age of advertisement and standardisation. And yet, this is a more enlightened age than any human beings have lived in hitherto. For instance, practically all of us can read. Some of you may say: "Ah! but what? Detective stories, scandals, and the sporting news." No doubt, compared with Sunday newspapers and mystery stories, the Œdipus, Hamlet and Faust are very small beer. All the same, the number of volumes issued each year continually gains on the number of the population in all Western countries. Every phase and question of life is brought more and more into the limelight. Theatres, cinemas, the radio, and even lectures, assist the process. But they do not, and should not replace reading, because when we are reading we can stop and *think,* and when we are just watching and listening somebody is taking very good care that we should not stop and think. The danger in this age is not of our remaining ignorant; it is that we should lose the power of thinking for ourselves. Problems are more and more put before us, but, except to cross-word puzzles and detective mysteries, do we attempt to find the answers for ourselves? Less and less. The short cut seems ever more and more desirable. But the short cut to knowledge is nearly always the longest way round. There is nothing like knowledge, picked up by or reasoned out for oneself.

Reading is the best corrective for the standardisation and the short-cut tendencies of this highly mechanised age. And reading enlarges one's acquaintanceship with the lives, natures and wants of other people; it is amazing how one can get out of oneself through books.

And that brings me to a serious point of philosophy, or shall we say the science of happy living.

For the great majority of people happiness depends on being thoroughly absorbed in what they are doing, feeling or thinking, moment by moment. When we are not carried out of ourselves, we are not really happy. I do not say we are actively unhappy while we're self-conscious; but we are only half alive. Tolstoi has told us that a man looking at himself in a mirror is not as nice-looking as he really is. How he made this shattering discovery we have yet to discover; for like most of Tolstoi's philosophical conclusions it is not so easy as all that. All the same: To forget self is the key to happiness. And there are all sorts of ways of forgetting self. A celebrated surgeon of my acquaintance began the process as a boy by giving his school-fellows ten cents apiece to let him pull their teeth out.

Politicians also are notoriously happy.

Yes, there are endless ways of forgetting self; and one of them is the contemplation of beauty. How lost was I when I first looked on the Grand Canyon of Arizona; when I first saw Isadora Duncan's child dancers; or the Saint-Gaudens' Adams memorial statue in Rock Creek cemetery at Washington; or the Egyptian desert under the moon.

But I should be the last to deny that forgetfulness of self may produce very curious results. A painter friend of mine was once so lost in painting a Russian dancer, that he painted her from the waist up with her face to himself, and from the waist down with her back to himself, and exibited the picture. But then he was, at the time, an Expressionist.

Let me come back to Life.

One does not ask even a scientist what Life is. The origin of Life is as much beyond our fathoming as is the nature of the Universe. We can speculate, and make countless deductions about existence, up to a point; but our speculations and deductions will never lead us to entire understanding. That is the one quite certain piece of knowledge. And who would wish it otherwise? Without the unknown the game of Life is nothing worth. With the everlasting riddle answered, all would become static, there would no longer be a Universe—no you, no I, no anything. Faith is not confined to the creeds of set religion. The best of all faiths is belief in the will towards Perfection operating in all that has ever been, is now, and ever shall be. Anyone who has that faith, wants to take part in the process of Perfection. Capable of seeing beauty, he feels he must try and contribute beauty; having a sense of proportion, he feels he must order his own goings in accordance with that sense. And wherever beauty and proportion guide us, the whole of human society benefits; moving ever further away from the quagmires into which greed and violence lead. One might take endless phases of Life to illustrate the need for the love of beauty and proportion. Let me take the question of Peace. That it should be a question at all seems farcical to one

with any love of beauty and proportion. The Great
War showed us havoc and death such as the world
had not yet seen. But owing to the development of
flying and poison gases, the havoc of the Great War
was child's play to the ruin implicit in any future
war between great nations. Given the conditions
under which any such war will be fought, the men,
women, and children of every partaking country
would seem to be doomed to creep—those who are
left—like rats in the drainpipes, or to flee distracted
like hares on a mountain. In wars of the future (if
there be such) there will be immediate attack from
the air on those nerve centres—the great towns—
from which no form of protection has been or is
likely to be discovered; they will be destroyed by
explosives or paralysed by gas bombs, and it seems
quite likely that armies and navies, dependent as they
are on these nerve centres, will hardly be used at all.
In wars of the future there will be nothing chival-
rous, nothing heroic, no honour, no glory; none even
of the mournful credits and excitement of the last
great war. No distinction between old and young,
between man, woman or child, between sick or
healthy; no immunity for religion or any form of
culture—nothing but gliding invisible shapes—a
murrain from the sky, death, sickness and desolation.
If there is not to be peace between the great so-called
civilised nations, then without exaggeration each
country that indulges in war (for a like fate will
befall all) will become as a shadow of itself and slink
into the pit of the Past.

284

This is no cry of alarm; it is but the warning of common sense.

There must come a change—they say—in human nature before wars can cease. There will be no such change in human nature. Cold-blooded, calculating men will always pursue their own gain; always there will be the narrow, blind, fanatical type of patriot; always weak men who let things drift till they are past control; and there will always be mob feeling.

But, there is improved machinery for the delay of warfare.

And there has come another saving difference in the general attitude towards war. In 1914 intelligent and sane men supposed (though they have been proved wrong) that war might bring real advantage to their countries; in 1930 no sane and intelligent man could entertain such a supposition. When a few hundred gas bombs tipped from a few machines can paralyse vast centres of population, no one in his senses could welcome war. Before 1914 to believe in the need for peace was to be something of a freak. In 1930 not to believe in the need for peace is to be a village idiot. That, again, is just common sense.

This is, indeed, a curious and poignant moment in the life of the human race. We live under a menace incomparably greater and more virulently savage than any menace in the most savage times of the past; and yet there has been no age hitherto that can be compared with the present for humane instinct and sincere desire to conquer the ills from which we human beings suffer. There is more knowledge, skill and humanity in the treatment of disease; more science, justice and mercy in our attitude towards criminals and in our conduct towards the animal world (though not yet by any means enough); and more earnest desire to remedy social and economic evils than there ever was before. If we can but assure peace, and lay this spectre of annihilation which hovers over us, we shall slowly reach the most benignant, just and prosperous age the world has yet known. It is impossible to exaggerate the benefit that would come to all our lives if we knew for certain that war among civilised nations was a nightmare of the past. And to my thinking there should never pass a day in the lives of any of us when we do not say to ourselves: "By the God that is in us— no more war."

Let me spend my few remaining minutes upon thought of beauty. Beauty means this to one person, perhaps, and that to the other. And yet when any one of us has seen or heard or read that which to him is beautiful, he has known an emotion which is in every case the same in kind, if not in degree; an emotion precious and uplifting. A choir-boy's voice, a ship in sail, an opening flower, a town at night, the song of the blackbird, a lovely poem, leaf shadows, a child's grace, the starry skies, a cathedral, apple trees in spring, a thoroughbred horse, sheep-bells on a hill, a rippling stream, a butterfly, the crescent moon—the thousand sights or sounds or words that evoke in us the thought of beauty—these are the drops of rain that keep the human spirit from

death by drought. They are a stealing and a silent refreshment that we perhaps do not think about but
which goes on all the time. The war brought a kind
of revolt against beauty in art, literature, and music,
a revolt that is already passing, and that I am sure
will pass. It would surprise any of us if we realised
how much store we unconsciously set by beauty, and
how little savour there would be left in life if it
were withdrawn. It is the smile on the earth's face,
open to all, and needs but the eyes to see, the mood
to understand.

And so I come back to my opening words about
Life. A man takes his ticket for the Unknown Station but once; or—to get away from mechanism in
this over-mechanical age—but once he starts forth
to walk his life through, under sun and rain.

We are all tramps when you come to think of it,
unknowing what the day will bring forth, or where
we shall sleep the night when it comes. If we can help
our neighbours, if we can keep our courage up, if
we can do our work well and with all our hearts, so
that we forget ourselves in doing it; if we can add to
beauty a little, if only by enjoying it; if we can seek
peace and ensue it; if we can look upon the face of
Mystery and yet feel the Spirit ever moving in this
our world of star-shine—we shall do well. Ah! we
shall do very well!

1930.

THE CREATION OF CHARACTER
IN LITERATURE

ROMANES LECTURE: 1931

THE CREATION OF CHARACTER
IN LITERATURE

THE whole question of character creation is mysterious, perhaps more mysterious to one who creates character than to those who smile or sniff under the creation; the process has no dossier, is devoid of documentation, and resists precise definition. Whether in literature or in life, creation has the same baffling inscrutability, and offers the same opportunities for talking without the book.

But the theme is chosen because its selector suspects, in common with not a few other people of the older fashion, that vitality of character creation is the key to such permanence as may attach to the biography, the play, and the novel.

Before coming, however, to the process of creation, it is well to touch on what may be called the 'make-up' of the creative mind. This lecturer is no philosopher—that being whom Oxford, with its tendency to Greek roots, brought one up to credit with a love of wisdom, but whom Life has forced one to conclude is rather a lover of intellectual exercise and the framer of conclusions where conclusion is unattainable. Considered over a wide enough span of time, philosophies are like the fashion of ladies' clothes, which appear absolute until by a new dash of the Parisian intellect they are shown to be relative.

Being no philosopher, then, this lecturer advances suspicions rather than conclusions. He suspects the substratum of the human being to be energy, or whatever the fashion of the moment calls it, identical with the energy of which everything else alive is made, so that it has basic touch with every other living thing, and sympathetically receives the impacts therefrom. Such impacts form that sum of experience which furnishes the individual's sub-conscious mind. In the human being those impacts are so infinitely many that we seem each of us to be a complete reservoir of sub-conscious experience, a secret storehouse of first-hand contacts, sights, sounds, scents, tastes, and of impressions at second-hand. If one can imagine the Catacombs at Rome, or the old cellars under the Adelphi, stored to the brim with photographic films, one has perhaps some notion of what the human sub-conscious mind is like. Every minute, every second indeed, of our existences adds to recorded experience stacked and piled and ready to be drawn on.

The lecturer, then, suspects that what we call our conscious or directive minds are normally only able to make a very limited and severely practical selective use of the treasures in our cellars, and that what we know as the creative gift in literature, or indeed in any art, is a more than normal power in certain people for dipping into the storehouse and fishing up the odds and ends of experience, together with a special aptitude for welding or grouping those odds and ends when they are fished up.

More fluidly, perhaps, one may think of the sub-conscious mind as a sort of lava of experience, over which the conscious mind has formed in a crust more or less thin, and more or less perforated by holes through which the lava bubbles. And we may think of what we loosely call creative genius as a much more than normal perforation of the crust, combined with a very high aptitude for shaping the emergent lava into the character of fiction, into pictures, music, or what not. So much, vaguely and tritely, for the make-up of the creative mind.

In considering the actual process of character creation, let us approach by way of its least mysterious, its recreative side—biography. Once on a time in that venerable and vocal institution for putting us in our right places—the Oxford Union—a certain brilliant biographer inaugurated a debate on 'the growth of superfluous biography.' Since we may be sure that he was not merely alluding to biographies not written by himself, we must suppose that he was thinking of those biographies which do not bring the dead to life. Possibly he proved his point, and birth control for biographers has since been established; but possibly not, for the creative instincts of literary folk are incorrigible. But let us assume, with him, that biography is only worth while if it creates, or rather re-creates character. Now, the task of a biographer is the clothing of a skeleton already in the cupboard; and, speaking from the creative point of view, the pre-existence of the skeleton is more than half his battle. The liberties which can be taken with enduring

and unmalleable bones, without incurring a sort of
Egyptian curse, are inconsiderable. A biographer may
crook a leg, leave out some teeth, or slightly curve
the spine, and still escape from Nemesis; the main
set and structure he must preserve or die violently.
A certain backbone of facts lies at the base of a task
which is perhaps more analogous to the creation of
character by a portraitist in oils than to the creation
of character by a writer of fiction. Having, then,
fetched his skeleton from its cupboard, dusted it,
and put it into a North light, the biographer will
proceed to drape on it muscle, tissue and skin, and
then such garments as may appeal to his æstheticism
or sense of decency, not always the same thing. From
innumerable documents, or the absence of them, he
will draw his clothing conclusions; and it will be seen
at once that his work is infinitely more concerned
with his conscious than with his sub-conscious mind.
That, indeed, is the second great difference between
the biographer and the novelist. The biographer is
throughout in conscious control, the novelist in conscious subjection to the sporadic irruptions of his
sub-consciousness. In an experimental epoch, such as
this, it has occurred to certain enterprising spirits to
attempt a blending of biography and fiction, and to
produce what may be called biographic plays or
novels. The figure of some one who has ruffled
through the past is taken, with a specious reverence
for certain facts, and clothed in fancy dress. The
result is frequently agreeable to the reader and pleasing to the pride and prejudice of the creator; but a

caveat should be entered. For if there be any value in history, as some people have been known to assert, this dressing-up of the sober dead, that they may dance to the pipes of fancy, is somewhat perilous. The historical novel has its dangers, as those well know who have read Dumas and rejected thereafter any mere *terre à terre* version of the French history of that period; but the biographic novel is more dangerous still. The historical novel is recognised from birth as a gay Lothario, but the biographic novel or play is a deliberate and subtle seducer in a Puritan's cloak. And one, who has ever preferred the plain cooking of fowls in their own flavouring juices to sauced-up versions, is bound to note, in passing, the will-o'-the-wisp quality of this particular form of character creation. The virtues in a biographer which most excite admiration are the industrious fidelity with which he unearths the significant relative minutiæ from the Long or Round barrows of history; and the lively but sober selective judgment with which he attaches them to the skeleton, framing out for our eyes an image which we feel to be as near the original as the biographer in limpid sincerity has been able to achieve. A biographer's temperament must in every case colour to some degree the re-created figure of his hero. But the less his temperament deviates the natural colours of the re-creation, the greater the achievement. In a sense the biographer's art is as much the art of criticism as of creation, and true criticism has a certain divine detachment, a devotion to truth, at the expense of, rather than to the gratifi-

cation of, the critic's self. This is why the good critic
and the good biographer are almost as rare as the
unicorn. The good biographer, like the good portraitist in oils, must be made of sponge and of steel.
All must he absorb, and all sieve, and then must have
at once constructive sympathy and resistant power
of the finest temper. Himself he must resist, curb
both his sense of the ludicrous, and his sentimental
impulses, yet withal keep warm and colourful. The
Public, past and present, he must resist—its prejudices and predilections. Even, as a rule, his publisher
and his own pocket he must resist. It is true that the
biographer has not, like the portrait-painter, to resist
the magnetic current emanating from one sitting in
a flesh which revolts from being unfavourably, or
shall we say truthfully, portrayed; but he has, not
uncommonly, to steel himself against the suscepti-
bilities of ancestor worship. In fact, when we con-
template the lions in the path of the biographer, we
need not wonder if he is sometimes eaten, and not
infrequently lost in the jungle. When looking at a
portrait by some Old Master, at Holbein's Sir
Thomas More or Rafael's Inghirami, where nothing
has been blinked, not even a wandering eye, and no
itch to startle or to innovate has been yielded to, one
feels what an instinctive and passionate reverence for
truth has animated the painter. The character that
he has brought to life out of his long and eager contemplation of the original compels from us a kind of
worship. We often hear the argument advanced—
indeed, one has advanced it oneself, for in this world

consistency is no more prevalent than the nightingale west of Exeter—that it does not matter whether a portrait is a portrait; the sitter will die and the picture remain, and nobody will know whether or not it was a good likeness, but only whether it is a good picture. That is perfectly true. On the other hand, if a portrait is not an attempt to re-create the sitter, why call it a portrait, and attach the sitter's name to it? Surely, on the whole, a portraitist is more sensibly governed by the re-creative adherence to truth which animates the best biographers; for he is at least as much tempted, by other considerations, to diverge. Vandyk—in many of whose portraits a certain agreeable composure, not unconnected with ruffles, is apparent, to the detriment of individuality—Vandyk we most admire when, as in his Petworth portrait of the Earl of Northumberland, he shakes himself free for the re-creation of the depths of character and mood. That picture is illustrative of the struggle between God and Mammon which perpetually engrosses portrait-painter or biographer. It was painted by Vandyk while Northumberland was languishing in the Tower. The bearded face is to one side, leaning on a hand, and the painter has imparted to it the long-suffering melancholy of prisoners and captives, together with the individual quality of the sitter. But even in this faithful picture, as if conscious of the dubious favour with which such a presentment of a nobleman would be received, Vandyk has restored confidence by placing the drooped figure against the background of a red velvet curtain, not precisely the normal garniture of prisons. Gazing at good portraits of people one has known best, one is ever more astonished at the deep reality and inwardness of being that can be revived for us by an artist who can feel, and see, and be faithful to his impressions. The same sort of true reflection is achieved in such a biographical study as Edmund Gosse's *Father and Son,* in George Trevelyan's Garibaldi books, in O'Brien's *Life of Parnell.* The secret of the best biography, as of the best portraiture, lies in a magical blending of sympathy and criticism. When Gainsborough painted his little daughters that they might dwell for ever catching butterflies, hand in hand, in summertime, he gave us a perfect illustration of the touching beauty that may breathe in the art of re-creation; when Boswell wrote his *Life of Johnson* he revealed to us the amazing possibilities of intimacy in that art.

Enough on a phase of character creation beyond the lecturer's personal experience. Let us pass, to trouble that at least he wots of—the creation of character as exemplified in plays and novels.

Some few years ago an industrious person, labouring in the vineyards of categorical knowledge, addressed a questionnaire to a number of well-known dramatists. He wished, lest there should be untidiness in this matter, to know exactly how they wrote their plays. Such answers as he received probably came from such as in writing plays fit characters to the plots thereof. And that, let it be said at once, is the chief pitfall before the dramatist, in so far as the creation of character is concerned. Is it conceivable that characters can live if pinned to the dictates of the set scenario? Admitting that a dramatist should know the trend and ending of his drama before he sits down to write it, he will be ill advised if he does not give his characters every chance to dictate to him, within that limit. For, even then, he is not so free as the novelist, and, if an inquiry were taken over the whole range of plays and novels, the surviving creations of character in novels would far outnumber those in plays. One might almost say that plays are recalled as plays, and novels by the characters in them. To a rule such as this there are outstanding exceptions, and those plays which have achieved real fame are usually associated with preeminent character creation. The conspicuous example of Shakespeare in this respect leaps to the eye. But Shakespeare had in him the makings of a great novelist before, as it were, the novel was born. Malory and the early romanticists come rather under the heading of fabulists; and, though Cervantes was Shakespeare's contemporary, the forms of expression in England at that time were emphatically the poem and the drama. Let us not, then, embarrass Shakespeare further by inscribing the word novelist on his chameleon's coat, lest we tempt some bright spirit to prove that Cervantes wrote him in his leisure moments by way of learning English. Unquestionably Shakespeare's greatest gift was his peerless command of words. He was, first and foremost, poet; but in character creation he certainly followed a brooding and whimsical method, served continually by the subconscious mind, far more symptomatic of the novelist than of the playwright. The instinctive looseness of his form is further evidence in the same direction. If Shakespeare had not chanced to be an actor, or at least intimately connected with dramatic enterprise, he might well have innovated the character novel in this country, and taken precedence of Cervantes as the first great realistic novelist. Shakespeare is the trump card of those who hold that, without an intimate and practical knowledge of the stage, no one can write an honest-to-God play. That is one of those half-truths which people are for ever desirous of converting into the whole. Its converse is the conviction that what is vital in the theatre comes into it on a side wind. Either rule can be proved speciously with the usual equivalent exceptions. The point is immaterial for the purpose of this address, but it brings one conveniently to the second great drawback to character creation in drama—the physical limitation, set by a stage, to the dramatist's creative freedom. A dramatist, of course, can let character hold sway and trust to luck—that is, indeed, the strength of the side-wind theory. But, though such disregard of the stage may forward the vitality of character creation, it will probably drive the producer to distraction. Almost inevitably the dramatist does think of this physical limitation. To think of it is called 'Obeying the rules of your medium,' and is the strength of the theory that close knowledge of the stage is essential to the writing of the real play.

Shakespeare certainly knew his medium, and, as certainly, disregarded it more freely than any one before or since. He can hardly be cited to prove anything. But, putting ourselves into the place of one who is trying to imagine a new being with the attributes and qualities of the full-blooded human creature, we shall soon see how galling and repressive it is to have to remember that our fancy man or woman can only do this or that owing to the limitations of a time and space which cannot be enlarged. Here, incidentally, is one of the advantages which the film has over the stage play; such an advantage, however, does not countervail the loss caused to the dramatist's creations by shadow representation, in place of representation by flesh and blood. And this brings up the third great drawback to character creation in plays. The dramatist cannot but be conscious that his characters are much at the mercy of their impersonators. Except perhaps in his first play, he will not easily avoid the feeling that, however intensely he may use his imagination, the imagined creature will not come out on the stage as he imagined it. There is no such thing as ideal casting; casting is a question of more or less right representation. And knowledge of this induces in the playwright a certain looseness of conception and workmanship in order that the garments of character may fit a greater selection of impersonators. Some dramatists are so acutely conscious of this particular limitation that they merely create rôles for selected players. This is to super-observe the rules of the medium in which they work, and the process cannot be dignified with the label 'character creation.'

The stage, in fact, inclines the creative writer to the fashioning of types rather than of individuals. Falstaff is perhaps the greatest exception to this rule. We think of the gorgeous old ruffian first and last as a private person, without attaching to him any particular phase of human character, as we attach violence to Lear, jealousy to Othello, unscrupulous decision to Lady Macbeth, and, wrongly perhaps, dreaming indecision to Hamlet. In the making of Falstaff—who, by the way, is very much a novelist's creation—Shakespeare gave full rein to his personal enjoyment, and from his enjoyment our own has been distilled. The subconscious mind had almost full command over the process; the sense of direction is lacking, or rather veiled from us. We might, indeed, label Falstaff "amorality personified"; but that is a literary afterthought. We swallow him first, huge morsel though he be, as we swallow life itself, amorphous and tasty, and ask for more.

One has called in doubt the type quality of Hamlet. Literary fashion takes him to be the antithesis of Don Quixote—as dreamer to knight errant; as man of thought to man of action. Does the text really bear out this convenient apposition? Hamlet is rather another illustration of a dramatist's surrender to the novelist's introspective and luxurious method, almost wholly controlled by the subconscious mind ministering to the creator's dominant mood at the moment. So subtle, so varied and elastic is the figure of Hamlet, that no one seems able to make a failure in the part. The great Hamlet, indeed, may be rare; the good Hamlet is a matter of course.

Let Hamlet bring us to the most fertile and important phase of this theme—the creation of character in novels.

This is without doubt the least trammelled and most subconsciously inspired form of character creation. The novelist needs but a quiet spot, some ink, some writing paper, and his own brooding energy to create that which may live but a season or endure for a century. Such complete independence renders his task at once the most attractive and yet the hardest and most mysterious. There are for him no adventitious aids, neither the handy skeleton, nor the unhandy sitter. No set scenes or dubious impersonators influence and deflect his imagination. In considering the process which the novelist follows, a question at once presents itself. Whence does he start? Does he consciously or subconsciously draw from life? Each novelist must answer that question in his own way, nor will his answer satisfy. Speaking as one who has been trying to write novels of character over a period of more than thirty years, the lecturer can make no real contribution to precision. To this day he knows not how he begins, or why, or how he goes on; he is only sure that there is no rule, and that the process of character creation varies not only from novelist to novelist, but even in himself. The nearest approach to a common formula may be attained in some such words as these: a real incident, or person, impinges sharply on a receptive mood of a novelist's particular nature or temperament; the thing observed and the mood of the observer click, as it were, like two cells clinging together to form the germ-point of creation. To this germ-point are attracted suitable impacts or impressions that have been stored in the subconscious mind, till the germ swells to proportions which demand the relief of expression, and in written words the novelist proceeds to free himself. The opening sentences describing a character are usually suggested by observation from life. If the observation be conscious the description will probably be altered very soon; but whether altered or not, the character will tend to diverge from the original model so rapidly that if the creator desire to keep to an observed type, he will have to resort continually to inbreeding by constant reintroduction of the original traits. That profound instinct for the breeding of blood-stock implanted in every English breast will assist us in understanding how a novelist, in the creation of his characters, selects certain salient human traits, and continually reinforces them; just as the blood-stock breeder selects certain strains of blood and gets as many crosses of them as he can without falling into the snare of too close inbreeding. But in spite of this breeding to type, everything done, or said, or felt by the character, when once it begins to live, will take it a little farther from the original model. And, normally speaking, this is what the novelist welcomes, because characters sedulously drawn from life are for obvious reasons undesirable. Turgenev, one of the most conscious yet exquisite of novelists, has left record of how he created the character of Bazarov. During a train journey he met, talked with, and observed a young doctor, who struck him as a new type. The journey—as journeys will—came to an end, and he never saw the young man again. But the impression on Turgenev was such that he set to work to conceive this young man's way of life and thought in the form of a diary. He kept this diary for months, as he imagined the young doctor himself might have written it, till he believed he knew how that young man would feel and act in all circumstances; he then began to write his novel *Fathers and Children,* making the young doctor, whom he named Bazarov, the principal character. Bazarov called himself a "Nihilist," an expression at once universally adopted to nickname the new type Russia was producing in those days. This example of highly conscious character creation stands out in thoroughness and direct motivity; but only a great selective artist could have followed with success so formal a method. The vitality and freedom of character creation derives, as a rule, from the subconscious mind instinctively supplying the conscious mind with the material it requires. In attempting an illustration of that process you must forgive my being personal for a moment. I sink into my morning chair, a blotter on my knee, the last words or deed of some character in ink before my eyes, a pen in my hand, a pipe in my mouth, and nothing in my

head. I sit. I don't intend; I don't expect; I don't
even hope. I read over the last pages. Gradually my
mind seems to leave the chair, and be where my
character is acting or speaking, leg raised, waiting
to come down, lips opened ready to say something.
Suddenly, my pen jots down a movement or remark,
another, another, and goes on doing this, haltingly,
perhaps, for an hour or two. When the result is
read through it surprises one by seeming to come
out of what went before, and by ministering to some
sort of possible future. Those pages, adding tissue
to character, have been supplied from the store-cup-
board of the subconscious, in response to the appeal
of one's conscious directive sense, and in service to
the saving grace of one's theme, using that word in
its widest sense. The creation of character, however
untrammelled and unconscious, thus has ever the
guidance of what, perhaps, may best be called "the
homing instinct."

An expression frequently used concerning books:
"The character of so and so took charge," is true
enough without being the whole truth. For a character can obviously never outrun the limits of his
"creator's" nature, nor take him beyond his secret
sense of shape. Even if that sense of shape be only
a glorification of the shapeless, it is still there, and
beyond it character will not set foot.

The case of Bazarov, already quoted, serves to
illustrate also the extremely intimate connection between character and story. Story in what we may call
the conscience-stricken novel is just character highly

and variously lit-up. Turgenev's theme in *Fathers and Children* is the apposition, and indeed opposition, of the younger to the older generation. His perception of a new type in the young doctor whom he met in the train supplied him not only with the desire to create the character of Bazarov, but with the theme or suitable environment in which to create him. The continual contrast between Don Quixote and Sancho Panza supplied Cervantes with the theme of his masterpiece. The plot of Turgenev's "Smoke" is wrapped into the form of the passion-inspiring Irina; the plot of Balzac's greatest novel into the doting figure of "Père Goriot." We cannot conceive the long romance of Dumas' Musketeer Series without the adventurous centrality of D'Artagnan's presence; of the *Pickwick Papers* without the benevolent presidency of Mr. Pickwick; or of Stevenson's *Kidnapped* and *Catriona* without the apposition between Lowlands and Highlands implicit in the forms of David Balfour and Alan Breck. But there is another side to this moon, well illustrated by that very great novel: Tolstoi's *War and Peace*. There, indeed, the panorama of life disclosed is so vast that even the leading characters seem subordinate. Nor has one the feeling in Tolstoi's other masterpiece, *Anna Karenina,* that the theme is more centred in Anna than in Levin.

Some early words in this lecture suggested that the permanence of a novel, a play, a biography, depends on the vitality of the characters therein. Let us narrow this issue down to the novel. Very few novels outlive their own generation; and of such survivors the majority live on merely as works dignified and popular in their time, the names on whose outsides are remembered, but whose insides are only examined by the scholar, or the person stranded in a remote hotel. The few novels of old times to which we still turn with gusto are almost always those in which a character or characters have outlived their period. How far would Thackeray be known to-day but for Becky Sharp, Major Pendennis, Colonel Newcome, Harry Foker, Esmond, Beatrice, and Barry Lyndon? How far would Trollope but for Mrs. Proudie? With Dickens we associate practically nothing now but a galleyful of strangely living creatures. George Eliot retains precarious foothold through her children, Silas Marner, Adam Bede, and Hetty. The character creations of Jane Austen still keep her memory fresh despite her unending parochialism. Except to the student of style Flaubert lives but in Madame Bovary and the old maid of "Cœur Simple." Fielding would be forgotten but for Tom Jones, Joseph Andrews, and Sophia. One can hardly indeed say that such books as *A Sentimental Journey, Cranford, Alice in Wonderland, Treasure Island,* and *Huckleberry Finn* survive by reason of character creation. They live mainly, and will ever live, from having been pickled in bright spirit. But such exceptions prove a rule which seems important to the future, because the last few years have shown a tendency in the novel to forsake individualism for a kind of communism; to abandon the drama of individual character, exhibited under high light and high pressure, in favour of a well-nigh scientific exposition of the species—human being: the feelings, thoughts, tendencies, foibles, and amenities of *homo* more or less *sapiens* are turned over and over for our inspection with amazing skill and industry, but without any intention to set him on his legs as an individual. The species as a whole has become the novelist's love, or object of detestation, rather than selected specimens of the species. The experiment is extremely interesting—especially to those who are making it. It has a vogue. And yet there are certain primary reasons why the creation of individual character as the chief motive and function of the novelist may never be adequately replaced by the pursuit of fine writing, verbal dialectics, vibrational reproductions of life, or even by these subtle expositions of the generalised human soul. There is, for instance, a deep craving in most of us to have interest in oneself from time to time replaced by interest in the self of another. This craving is satisfied by the creation of character in fiction much more frequently and soothingly than by real folks, even one's own friends and relatives. Again, most of us deeply crave to see ourselves reproduced, more or less, in the characters we read of, and to judge ourselves by them. Dissection of the generalised human being supplies us with information, but gives us no outline sharp enough for comparison with our own. The unending moral assessment which is so deep a part of the life of a human being is more furthered and furnished by the character creations of fiction than most of us realise. One could not say that consciousness of this should guide a novelist, for if it did he would make a failure of his characters. But, when his task is finished, it is always comforting to a novelist to know that by the creation of character he contributes to the organic growth of human ethics. If, indeed, a novelist has any use in the world apart from affording entertainment, it is through the revealing power of his created characters.

One has come to the run-in without hope of breasting the tape, for the inexplicable has still to be explained. What makes a character endure? Or conversely: What makes so many of them die? At the end of every publishing season fictional characters are bunched like autumn flies waiting to drop dead. Presently Time, the housemaid, comes round with a brush, sweeps them off the wall, opens the window and decants them into the winter jessamine. Many of them have died of being "interesting" or "strangely moving"—those convenient but fatal words! Some, too big for their boots, and harassed by corns, have rushed to a violent end. A few, not many nowadays, have perished of a surfeit of sugar. A considerable number, too fond of their creators, have fallen into religious ecstasy and committed *felo de se*. And the rest, having spent their days trying to collect themselves, have simply given it up.

In those few character creations which endure is a quality which can best, perhaps, be described as homespun yet vital; they are vivid from ever revealing themselves without seeming to. If one had to give the palm to a single factor in the creation of character, it would be to sly, dry humour. The sort of humour which produced the Don and Sancho, Falstaff, Major Pendennis, Becky Sharp, Sam Weller, Micawber, Betsy Trotwood, Stepan Arcadyevitch, and Mrs. Proudie. But such a quality is rather a shaping instrument than the mainspring of enduring character creation. What the mainspring itself is remains mysterious. Call it, if you will, vital spark, "breath of life." One thing is sure: The enduring characters in literature are ever such as have kicked free of swaddling clothes and their creators. Theirs is a sublime unconsciousness of the authors of their being. They toddle and strut, and hale you with them into the streets, the fields, the sands, and waters of their private pilgrimages, that you may see their stars and share their troubles, laugh with them, love with them, draw with them the breath of their defiances, suffer in their struggles, float out with them into the unconscious when their night comes.

1931.

THE END

DATE DUE

#47-0108 Peel Off Pressure Sensitive